Days We Remember

Days We Remember

Momentous Events in Irish Life

DEIRDRE PURCELL

HACHETTE
BOOKS
IRELAND

Copyright © Deirdre Purcell 2008

First published in 2008 by Hachette Books Ireland

The right of Deirdre Purcell to be identified as the Author of the Work has been asserted by her in accordance with the Copyright, Designs and Patents Act, 1988.

1

A CIP catalogue record for this title is available from the British Library.

ISBN 978 0 340 97793 4

Typeset in Sabon 12pt by Sin É Design
Cover and interior design by Sin É Design
Printed and bound in Italy by L.E.G.O Spa.

Hodder Headline Ireland's policy is to use papers that are natural, renewable and recyclable products and made from wood grown in sustainable forests. The logging and manufacturing processes are expected to conform to the environmental regulations of the country of origin.

Hachette Books Ireland
8 Castlecourt Centre
Castleknock
Dublin 15, Ireland

A division of Hachette Livre UK Ltd.,
338 Euston Road, London NW1 3BH, England

Previous:

Dana's Eurovision song contest win with 'All Kinds of Everything', 1970.

Bono says 'Yes' to the Good Friday Agreement: on stage with David Trimble and John Hume, 1998.

'You did it again!' Terry Phelan hugs Ray Houghton, Giants Stadium, World Cup, June 1994.

Devastation on Remembrance Day, Enniskillen, 1987.

Contents

Also by Deirdre Purcell

Non-Fiction

Follow Me Down To Dublin

Diamonds and Holes in my Shoes

Be Delighted: A Tribute to Maureen Potter

On Lough Derg (with photographer, Liam Blake)

The Time of My Life (ghostwriter for Gay Byrne)

The Dark Hunger (with photographer, Pat Langan)

Fiction

Tell Me Your Secret

Children of Eve

Last Summer in Arcadia

Marble Gardens

Entertaining Ambrose

Love Like Hate Adore

Sky

Francey

Falling for a Dancer

That Childhood Country

A Place of Stones

Screenplay

Falling for a Dancer (for BBC and RTE)

Open Door adult literacy series

Jesus and Billy are off to Barcelona

Has Anyone Here Seen Larry?

Short Story contributions

Ladies Night At Finbar's Hotel

Moments

Irish Girls Are Back in Town

This book is dedicated to my niece and godchild Gillian Purcell,

with deep admiration for her courage and altruism.

Introduction

Did you see the Pope when he came to Ireland in 1979? But how did that weekend go for Bishop John Magee, who was looking at us from over Pope John Paul's shoulder?

Maybe you remember the day in 1988 when Ray Houghton shot the ball into the back of the England net in Stuttgart? How did that feel for him?

Have you ever wondered, as I have, how, throughout Holy Week in 1998, Bertie Ahern managed his parallel lives – the first involving critical, last-chance negotiations of the Good Friday Agreement, the second seeing him commute daily between Hillsborough and the obsequies surrounding the death of his mother in Dublin?

The episodes for this book have been chosen because of my own curiosity – and from interest in the uncommon individuals interviewed. The only criterion for each was that it might stimulate readers' own recall; I make no claim to deal comprehensively with

Previous:
Riverdance
at the Apollo
Theatre, London.
Breandán de Gallai
and Joanne Doyle
with members of
the cast.

Opposite: Putting
on the Ritz for the
Holy Guest – visit
of Pope John Paul
II, 1979.

any one event, certainly not with the period in question from the early seventies right up to May 2008, because there was far too much from which to choose.

In addition to the triumphal events that united us, and the scandals, atrocities, crimes, frauds, abuses and controversies that divided us, we mourned the Tuskar, Air India and 'Beaujolais' plane crashes, other fatal air, road, fire, rail and marine incidents, and far too many murders and murder-suicides. While our hearts still go out to the families whose loved ones have vanished without trace, we also continue to speculate about the disappearance of Shergar. I could not cover more than a fraction of it all.

So, here, in addition to the recollections of Bertie, Ray and the Bishop, are the experiences of Tom McSweeney, who covered the train crash at Buttevant and the blowing apart of the oil tanker *Betelgeuse*. We can never forget the horrific bombings at Omagh, Dublin, Monaghan or Enniskillen, the latter recalled here through the heart-rending experiences of that deeply Christian man, the late Gordon Wilson. Here, too, is the tragedy that unfolded during one St Valentine's night at the Stardust Nightclub. And, although the catastrophe at Hillsborough football stadium happened offshore, I have included it because it transfixed us.

On the happier side of the scale, Charlie McCreevy reveals the genesis and consequences of his SSIA wheeze – remember that? And remember Gillian Bowler's 'Budget Bum' poster for Budget Travel, the company that, in our pre-Ryanair world of grey drizzle, gloom, and financial scrimping, shook up the travel scene and made package holidays accessible, fun and exciting.

While there is no Ronnie Delany (Ronnie has written his own terrific memoir), Eamon Coughlan, Eddie Macken, John Treacy or Sonia O'Sullivan, here is Christy O'Connor Junior whose two-iron shot on the 18th (and the one at the 17th that 'nobody saw') at the

Belfry was, for Europe, pivotal in wresting the Ryder Cup from its temporary U S resting place.

Bill O'Herlihy remembers Italia '90 while also exposing shy but staunch personal beliefs. Johnny Logan remembers those innocent days before we all became sophisticated and too jaded to treat the Eurovision Song Contest as irony or with derision. And Moya Doherty, who rarely grants interviews, outlines her creation of *Riverdance*, that phenomenon which, like a dazzling Catherine wheel, continues to roll around the world.

And what can anyone say about the irrepressible Mike Murphy? He had to be included for the number of times he lightened our darkest days with his cheery on-air company.

Finally, a word about RTÉ in general and Gay Byrne in particular.

While not by design, the national broadcaster does seem frequently to crop up in this book. Before Newstalk, Today FM, LMFM, TV3 et al grew the teeth effectively to chomp their way through the national broadcaster's dominance, the old warhorse was the only game in town during many of the occurrences referred to here.

As for your host, Gay Byrne, I had asked to talk to him about the lonely death of fifteen-year old Ann Lovett and her baby son at a Marian shrine in Granard, Co Longford, because it had been reported so superbly on his radio show. In the course of the session with him, however, it transpired that the Ann Lovett story, sad though it was, was not foremost in his memory. Hers was just one narrative in the massive compendium of significant broadcasts during his long reign on radio and television. And so his name will surface more than once.

There was one person, though, whom even Gay could not nab, because he, like virtually the entire population of Ireland, knew that when Pope John Paul II came to this country the man would be too busy to fit him in.

Ireland's Alleluia Weekend

John Paul II in Ireland

It is a beautiful morning in Cobh.

In dread of being less than punctual (boarding school, acting and broadcasting training) I am more than two hours early. It is still only a quarter to nine and my appointment with the Bishop of Cloyne is for eleven o'clock.

I kill time in the hotel opposite the bishop's residence. Talk about location, location, location – the house sits on a sloping cliff opposite Cobh's great cathedral. On this warm May day, the terraces of both buildings overlook a calm, glittering sea in which Spike Island floats, innocent of its penal past.

Bishop John Magee and I are to meet to discuss a September weekend in 1979. Remember that weekend? When on the Friday, if you were within any sort of reasonable distance of Dublin city, you

Pope John Paul touches the forehead of Paul Kelly (14) of Dublin during a meeting with handicapped children at Cabra Convent.

set out in the early hours – maybe as early as three or four a.m., with food and flask, cushion, blanket and camping stool to join the rivers of people already approaching the Phoenix Park from every direction.

In that park, a wide, grassy area had been fenced into corrals in front of an edifice as big as an ocean liner, surmounted by a new 116-foot-high cross. This was the altar from which Pope John Paul II was to make his first address to the Irish nation. Music for the Mass, concelebrated by himself with one hundred and fifty cardinals, bishops and priests, was sung and played by the Garda and Army Number One bands, Our Lady's Choral Society, the late tenor Frank Patterson, mezzo-soprano Bernadette Greevy – always the woman for the big occasion – and six thousand voices from Dublin choirs.

These facts don't transmit the totality of what happened that weekend. 'One lady,' says the bishop, 'wrote to me afterwards. "People were sharing," she said. "Chairs. Food. The whole country was on the move during Ireland's Alleluia Weekend."' The bishop's face softens with remembering it. The décor in his sunny, high-ceilinged drawing room, windows framing views of the cathedral and that shining sea, is old-fashioned but elegant.

As one of the late Pope's private secretaries, John Magee's job had been to help with the preparations for the visit, to accompany his boss every step of the way, and afterwards to help to deal with the 240,000 thank-you letters received from Ireland by the Vatican.

On behalf of John Paul II, Monsignor Magee, as he was then, replied not only to the Alleluia letter, but to as many more as he could manage, including one from a lady in Knock. She had been among the earliest to arrive at the shrine to claim her place by a barrier beside which, she had been assured, the Pope would pass. He didn't, for logistical reasons: the programme was overrunning by hours and the scheduled 'drive-about' in the Popemobile, through the crowd of 450,000, was severely curtailed.

In her letter, the woman thanked John Paul for coming, but she also told him how disappointed she had been because she had 'hoped and prayed' that she would get to see him at close quarters. She was small, she wrote, and was able to see him only in the distance. But she had comforted herself, she added, with the thought, 'Wasn't I privileged to be standing on the same ground as the Vicar of Christ?' (Not everyone was so forgiving: there were grumblings from Knock about Bishop Eamonn Casey, who had encouraged the lengthening of the ecstatic youth celebrations in the previous venue, Galway.)

The logistical problem was that the Pope, running late in any event, and moved by the sight of so many of the sick who had waited for hours simply to be in his presence, had lingered too long in the Basilica – so long that, outside, 'it was getting dark and the helicopter

The Pope mobile.

crew was threatening not to fly. They were getting close to being out of hours. We were rushed straight from the Mass into the helicopter, otherwise we would have been grounded for the night in Knock.'

Apart altogether from its spiritual significance, the country was ripe for a massive outpouring of communal joy. Unemployment, emigration, punitive interest rates and high taxes were the stuff of life, so any excuse to relieve the unremitting gloom by joining in any national festival was to be grabbed with both hands. The magnitude of this one, vested on the shoulders of this handsome, exotic, charismatic and physically strong figure, whose obvious holiness was seemingly allied to a fresh, outward-looking view on the secular world, cannot be overstated.

Officially, the Irish state, its agencies and semi-state bodies strained resources to make the three-day occasion as memorable as possible. A special postage stamp was commissioned, prisoners were given amnesties, CIE threw out its normal schedules to facilitate transport; the Gardaí and army drew up detailed but relatively discreet security, crowd-management and contingency plans.

Newspapers printed how-to-get-there maps to the venues. The lay population rowed in: voluntary marshals and organisers, many from the GAA, appeared in their thousands to act as stewards for the vast crowds. RTÉ rose to the occasion with blanket coverage from outside-broadcast units, while large-screen TV monitors were erected so that, for example, while she waited for him along with her 449,999 fellow pilgrims, our small lady in Knock could alleviate the boredom of her many hours' waiting by watching what was happening at other locations.

By the time the Pope left us he had delivered nine major speeches to two-thirds of the Irish population. One and a quarter million people heard him in the Phoenix Park at a time when a quarter of a million more were already waiting for him at Killineer beside the

Dublin–Belfast Road. To come were the throngs at Clonmacnoise, Galway, Knock, Maynooth and Limerick.

Let's go back a little to find out how an Irishman from Newry, who was within a few feet of John Paul II's white cassock during every moment of his Irish visit, came to be so close to a Polish pope.

As a member of the Vatican Secretariat and a fluent Italian speaker, Father Magee had been chosen by one of John Paul II's predecessors, Pope Paul VI, as a secretary. And after Paul's death, Pope John Paul I took him on for his own short reign.

He tells an eerie tale about John Paul I. John Magee (there are a lot of Johns in this story) was standing beside John Paul I during the first general audience he had given in the Vatican's audience hall after his installation. 'And after that audience he went down to the *prima fide*, the front row, where there was a large group of Mexican journalists. One of them handed him a facsimile of an airline ticket – with his name and route filled in: Rome to Puebla, dated for February of the following year, 1979. This was a trip, originally planned for Paul VI that had remained on the papal schedule. On the way back to the apartment, just myself and himself in the car with the driver, he said to me, "Where is that ticket?"

'"Holy Father," I said, "it's not a ticket, it's a facsimile."

'"I know. But give it to me."

'So I gave it to him. He looked at it and handed it back to me and said: "I will never travel outside Rome. I will not travel to any foreign country. Give that to my successor. My successor will go to Puebla."'

The certainty of the Pope's tone startled John Magee, who remains convinced that the man had a clear premonition of his death. 'This was the first intimation. It was the first of a whole series of statements he made to me that made it clear he knew he was going to die. He had bad blood circulation and was conscious of his health but he definitely had a premonition.' And Albino Luciano did die, on 28 September

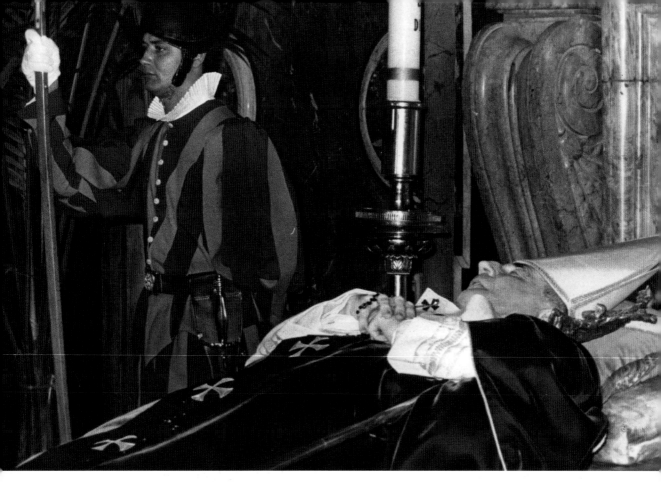

1978, just 34 days after his coronation, having served in the shortest pontificate since Leo XI in 1605.

His death spawned a thousand conspiracy theories, including murder: he had been poisoned because he had planned to make changes within the Vatican and the Curia, its religious bureaucracy. The rumours grew because there had been no autopsy. Because John Magee had been very close to John Paul, had had dinner with him on the evening before he died and, it was alleged, had found the body, he became entangled in the rumours, which were publicised widely in the world's press.

Had he been named in this context?

'Yes.'

They alleged you actually poisoned him?

'Yeah – it was terrible . . . ' He hesitates, searching for something less painful to discuss.

He had indeed been the first officially to 'find' the corpse of John Paul I, but in fact the discovery of the Pope's death had been made by a nun. That morning, on seeing that the cup of coffee she left each day outside the Pope's bedroom door had remained untouched, she knocked on the door. When there was no response, she entered the room.

At first the Vatican suppressed this terrible fact. A nun? A woman? Seeing a Pontiff in his pyjamas?

In *His Holiness*, their biography of John Paul I, journalists Carl Bernstein and Marco Politi include two snippets that confirm Bishop Magee's convictions about Luciano Albino's premonitions. The first concerns a statement he had made a few days before he died in which he told the Vatican's Secretary of State that his successor had been sitting in front of him during the conclave at which he himself had been elected. That man had been Karol Wojtyła. 'He will come,' said John Paul I, 'and I will go.'

The second concerns that last dinner. As they finished, John Paul said to Magee: 'I've made all the arrangements for the spiritual exercises next Lent. The retreat I'd like to make now is the retreat for a good death.'

Bishop Magee believes that the reason his own was the 'very first appointment' of Karol Wojtyła's pontificate was tied to the murder allegations: 'When he was coming out of the conclave and going to the apartment, he was about to break the seal when he turned to the Archbishop beside him and said, "Get me the Irish secretary."'

When 'the Irish secretary' entered the papal apartment at five o'clock that afternoon, he found the Pope 'sitting at the desk I used to occupy. He stood up, walked across, embraced me and said, "Now you stay with me!" That was my appointment!

'There had been so much press speculation, he insisted that I would be with him all the time to put an end to that. He said to me, "I want you by my side to make it quite clear that you had nothing to do with it." He was a most considerate man.' In this sunny drawing room, the strain of having been the subject of those allegations is evident three decades after the events. (There was also a pedestrian reason for his appointment: Monsignor Stanislaw Dziwisz, the secretary who had been with the new Pope for years in Krakow, at that time spoke no English and very little Italian.)

This Wojtyła proved to be very sociable. 'I was at his table. Paul VI would have had just his two secretaries at his table – he wouldn't have had any visitors. Pope John Paul I began the practice of inviting people to his table, family, friends and so on.

'John Paul II expanded that enormously. He would invite different nationalities, and whoever sat directly opposite him was the arbiter of which language, German, French, Spanish, we used that night. If there was anyone present who didn't understand that language, he would stop the conversation and translate it himself. He would put beside me a person who could speak either English or Italian. And he would stop the conversation every so often and say to that person, "Now, you tell John what we have been talking about."'

Very early on when breakfasting with his new boss, 'the Irish secretary' produced the Mexican facsimile air ticket and recounted its provenance. 'And the Holy Father said, "Yes, that's for Mexico. There are only three countries I would like to visit during this first year, Mexico, Poland and Ireland. Because they are the three countries to which I wish to give the title *semper fidelis*. Mexico maintains a great devotion to Our Lady and the Church, and to the See of Rome. Poland the same. And Ireland. I have longed always to go to Ireland. Now I am getting the opportunity."'

So he came, on 29 September, on board the *St Patrick*, Aer Lingus's flagship jumbo, his coat of arms freshly painted on the fuselage.

To have him and his group on board was a major coup for the

national airline. It had managed, with considerable difficulty, to wrest its VIP from the hands of Alitalia by offering to fly the papal entourage and accompanying press for free from Rome to Dublin and then, also gratis, to carry the much-augmented group onwards from Shannon to Boston for a visit to the US.

There hadn't been much time to prepare, so the *St Patrick* had been withdrawn from commercial service to undergo a special mechanical once-over – and a spectacular refurbishment of the cabin. A posh bed sit was installed on the upper deck, the décor of which included a handmade wooden crucifix, seats upholstered in yellow and white – and a large bed dressed with white Irish linen and a yellow tweed blanket. To be sure, to be sure, a second 747, with a round-the-clock reserve crew on standby, was similarly kitted out. And, to be sure, to be sure, to be sure, a trusty old 707 was ready and waiting in the background.

Door-stepping the Pope on the jumbo St Patrick.

9

These aircrafts' crews had been hand-picked to incorporate nursing and linguistic skills. (And I have it on good authority that many of the stewardesses who boarded the *St Patrick* that day were carrying bagfuls of rosaries, scapulars, holy pictures and other items for their distinguished passenger to bless.)

Breakfast aboard that morning for the Holy Guest and his inner circle was the Full Irish, served on a table with a centrepiece of red roses and laid with white linen napery, bone china and Waterford crystal. By all accounts, he lorried into the food – with special praise for the black pudding. After breakfast he took an unscheduled wander down to the steerage cabin to talk to journalists, some less appreciative than others because, Pope or no Pope, they were busy. Aer Lingus had allowed RTÉ engineers to install a transmitter in the body of the aircraft and had dedicated one of the 747's transmission channels to it so that a minute-by-minute broadcast could take place during the last few minutes of the trip, a world first from a commercial airliner. His Holiness approached this set-up and asked what was going on. 'It's RTÉ Radio,' said the harassed reporter, whose focus was to get his commentary through.

John Paul didn't take the hint. Curious, he persisted: 'What is RTÉ Radio?'

'Ireland's public-service broadcasting station,' snapped the reporter.

'God bless Irish radio!' John Paul had a sense of humour.

When the jumbo reached Irish airspace, 30 miles east of Courtown, it was joined at 18,000 feet by an escort of Fouga fighters from the Irish Air Corps. The crews had orders to shoot at any unauthorised aircraft but nobody need have worried. Bishop Magee loves this next bit: 'We had been going over his talk for the Phoenix Park so I could correct some of his pronunciation, but once the two fighter jets came alongside, one on each side, I said, "Holy Father! Look!" We could see the pilots through the right-hand window and the left-hand window.

'He blessed them. '

You may have guessed what's coming – you'd be spot on. Right and left, the pilots responded. 'We could see them blessing themselves. And I said, "Holy Father, let them alone! They're travelling at such speed!"'

The big aircraft, with its screaming escort, descended to an altitude of just a thousand feet and then, having made a turn above the entrance to Dublin Port, flew along the course of the River Liffey as far as the Phoenix Park where it banked again. When it was directly over the crowd, the captain dipped a wing to starboard so that the Pope could see the ground below. One person on board that day says he will never forget the sight of all the tightly packed waving hands below, 'like leaves on trees blowing in the wind'.

The owners of those hands maintain to this day that the captain's extraordinary gesture remains one of the most dramatic few seconds they have ever witnessed. They continue to describe to their children – and now grandchildren – their surprise and delight at the sight of the majestic aircraft's unexpected appearance in the sky so low and directly overhead. How one of its giant wings dipped in recognition of their presence. How they felt when they realised that the Pope's visit to their country was actually happening: that he was in that jumbo jet. That he was seeing them. That they were close enough to see his hand, in its white sleeve, at one of the aircraft's upper windows. They hadn't imagined this. 'When the captain announced that we were coming over the Phoenix Park, the Pope got up and went to the window and looked down. We could see them all. It was a magnificent sight, spread out underneath.'

And then the air hostess made the PA announcement of her career. The bishop repeats it with relish: '"Your Holiness, Your Eminences,

members of the Papal entourage, ladies and gentlemen, please return to your seats and fasten your seatbelts. We are about to land at Dublin airport."

'I was standing in the aisle and as he came towards me to get back to his seat I said, "Holy Father, welcome to my country!" And he put his arms around me and he said, "John, my long desire has been fulfilled. I have come to Ireland." For me it was a very emotional moment.'

From the instant the jumbo landed, the Pope's Irish schedule began to groan under the weight of events packed into it. Those planning it had seriously underestimated the visit's impact, the size of the crowds and the extent of their sustained reaction. 'And his reaction to them too. We considered that the enthusiasm of the Mexican crowd was to be taken for granted. His visit to his own people in Poland? The reaction there was to be understood too . . .' But that expected in Ireland had been placed in a different category: 'It was thought almost to be a Nordic country and so the enthusiasm was out of all proportion to what we had expected. He was behind all the time. The programme and the pace and the shortness of the visit – it was killing.' So much so that, as they went from venue to venue, John Magee's boss frequently turned to him: '"John, how many people are there in Ireland?" He was certainly overwhelmed. All of us were. He said to me later on, "You know the only place they tried to kill me? It was in Ireland!"

[This, of course, was before the attempted assassination on his own doorstep.] The Papal visits became streamlined after that one.'

I ask about the odd gesture John Paul II seemed to make in response to the cheering and applause he encountered at every stop. He didn't wave, throw his arms wide, or take the applause like the trained actor he was but, hands cupped in front of his chest, made small, upward-pumping movements.

Magee smiles mischievously: 'It was to encourage them. "More! More! Bravo! More!"'

John Paul was distressed, however, when he found he would be more than two hours late for two Dublin meetings with the Irish cabinet and with journalists, mixed with representatives of other churches and diplomats. Because of his Eastern European background, he was shrewdly cognisant of the power of the free media. 'I can't appear before them so late,' he said to the bishop, on the way to the Dominican convent in Cabra. 'All I can say is *mea culpa, mea culpa . . .*'

Previous: Aerial view of the crowd, Phoenix Park, Dublin.

'And I said, "Holy Father, your talk has already been distributed. So all you have to do is appear."'

So that was what he did. The journalists had been waiting in a room over which 'there was a kind of balcony. I remember he came out on that. And the first thing he did was . . .' Bishop Magee demonstrates. The supreme leader of millions of Roman Catholics around the world beat his breast in sorrow and humble apology in front of a bunch of Irish and foreign journalistos.

And what did they do? They burst into 'For He's A Jolly Good Fellow'.

At the end their guest, clearly taken aback, said, 'You say that I am a jolly good fellow – and I keep you waiting more than two hours?'

They sang it again.

'He always remembered that. It was the one time in his life when journalists sang to him.'

The formidable Chicagoan Archbishop Paul Marcinkus was the burly prelate in charge of the overstretched logistics. He also acted as the Pope's unofficial minder: by one account, when a too-persistent reporter was racing past his aircraft seat in pursuit of the Pope, he was observed to deliver an elbow in the groin.

On the last morning, when fog threatened a long delay, Marcinkus ordered that a visit to Maynooth should be cancelled. 'John,' he said to his Irish secretary, 'I think we have to go straight to Limerick.'

'We can't,' the Irishman objected. 'The heart of the church is in Maynooth.' The seminarians were waiting in the college chapel and in all, inside and out, the crowd numbered fifty thousand, including massed clergy and missionary societies. But what was concerning Marcinkus was that the flight from Shannon to Boston should leave 'at exactly the time scheduled so it would arrive exactly on time. The Americans thought Ireland was just a stopover on the way to them.'

John Magee wasn't having it. He went over the Archbishop's head to the boss and Maynooth stayed in, with the schedule adjusted to cut out the chapel. The seminarians were moved outside to join the crowd.

We don't know if the Pope saw the white nappy being waved up at him from a Leixlip garden as his helicopter, 40 minutes behind schedule, passed overhead. But when his party landed in the grounds of the college, along with Cardinal Ó Fiaich and Monsignor Horan, Maynooth's president, we do know that the Popemobile was whizzed straight towards the chapel in accordance with the original timetable. The Archbishop tried to divert it but the driver, under instruction from Monsignor Horan, ignored him and drove doggedly on.

And here comes the understatement of the trip: 'Marcinkus became annoyed.' Apparently Cardinal Ó Fiaich instructed him to take it easy.

In the chapel, meanwhile, the seminarians, keyed up and unaware of any drama outside, had been getting impatient and, drowning the flute of James Galway, had started to chant: 'We want the Pope! We want the Pope!' Then, even more daringly, they broke into song. The Pope had the 'whole world' in his capable hands. By the time he did arrive, they were so excited they reacted like kids meeting Santa Claus.

Bishop Magee travelled the world with John Paul II, 64 trips in all. They last travelled together in 2000 when the Pope's health was beginning to fail.

The final time they spoke, they were reminiscing: '"I suppose," he said to me, "the most memorable visit from your point of view was our trip to Ireland?"

'"Yes," I said. "But it wasn't the best organised from the point of view being rushed."

'"The pace!" he said. "And trying to keep up with the programme – but I will never forget."

'In particular, the visit to Galway always remained with him. They wouldn't stop singing and there were some people who wanted to quieten them, but he said, "No, no! Let them. Young people need to be able to express their feelings."'

At general audiences in St Peter's Square, there is always a lot of noise, with various groups and pilgrimages trying to attract the Pope's attention by waving flags and calling out their individual nationalities. In the melee, John Paul always found it difficult to distinguish 'Irlanda' from 'Islanda' (Iceland) or 'Ollanda' (Holland), 'so I told any groups I'd met to shout, "Galway!" and he'd always turn to them. His encounter with the youth of Ireland was the beginning of a world encounter. He decided that from then on, any visit he made would have an official youth element.'

There were two omissions on the Pope's itinerary in 1979. One was Armagh, where he had been determined to go, despite warnings from security people and governments both north and south. 'We had it on the programme. And I remember that on the morning when the news came through about the killing of Lord Mountbatten, his immediate reaction was, "Now I must go to Armagh. This is a tragic situation. I must be there!"' His determination increased with the news of the British soldiers killed in Warrenpoint a couple of days later, and the authorities had 'some task' to convince him that this would be a bad idea. He gave up 'only when they said, "You will be all right – it's the people around you. The crowd. Anything, a bomb, anything can happen in a crowd. And are you to allow your whole visit to be overshadowed by a tragedy?"'

The other omission was not an omission at all, but perceived as such by the people of Sean MacDermott Street in Dublin, who had somehow got it into their heads that John Paul would drop by their church to pray at the tomb of Matt Talbot, the Dublin working man and reformed alcoholic, locally venerated as a saint. Perhaps word had got out that John Paul II was devoted to Talbot because he had written about him.

All three popes with whom Bishop Magee served had evinced 'a great devotion' to Matt Talbot. Each would apparently have furthered his cause 'but the miracle hasn't come. I remember Paul VI saying to me, "You can have all the devotion, but if the local people don't have an attachment to the cause, there won't be a miracle and he will not be canonised."'

As the papal cavalcade passed the church in Sean MacDermott Street, 'he did notice all the big banners. He turned around to

Matt Talbot: no miracles, so no canonisation – despite the Pope's admiration.

Marcinkus to ask him if he could stop and Marcinkus said, "No, we can't . . ." I agreed. It would have been chaos. He would have been mobbed. We wouldn't have been able to handle it. It was never in the programme.'

Magee and John Paul II were musing one day about what they could do for Matt, 'and he said, "The conversion of Matt Talbot, and the grace that followed, wasn't that the miracle?"' John Magee had to remind him that rules were rules and that any candidate for sainthood had to be dead and perform a miracle as a 'sign from heaven'. He is convinced that John Paul II will soon be canonised because at the moment of the Pope's death, there was a miraculous curing – now undergoing verification – of a dying French nun.

Next page: Crowd alongside the Pope's cavalcade through the city.

'It was not in his nature to say no. I came to learn the quality of that man. Every evening, after a gruelling day of adulation, a day of sharing his life with everybody, he would come back to his residence and the first place he would go to would be the chapel to prostrate himself before the Tabernacle. Every day.

'When you'd see him like that, you would realise what an intimate relationship he had with the Lord.'

Somehow they got through the Irish programme as set out, and were on time leaving for Boston – and, like John F. Kennedy, John Paul planned to come back. 'When we were leaving Shannon, they were singing' – Bishop Magee sings, he has a fine voice – '"Will Ye No' Come Back Again?" He turned to me and said, "I will come back."'

Also like Kennedy, he never did.

Does the bishop miss the late Pope?

'I miss him very, very much. I loved him. He was a father to me and a brother . . .'

The cross that hangs around the bishop's neck 'was commissioned to commemorate the twenty-fifth year of his pontificate. He gave it to me personally.' He takes off the heavy gold ring he wears, to show, engraved inside, the Pope's name and his coat of arms. 'He had ten of them minted for the Jubilee Year, 2000, and this is the first of the ten. He put this on my finger.'

There is also another memento, the most precious of all.

On the night before Karol Wojtyła died, the phone rang in the bishop's house in Cobh. The call was from Monsignor Dziwisz, the Polish secretary. 'He said, "John, come quickly, the Holy Father is going."

'I immediately tried to get a flight but I couldn't get one until the Sunday morning.' When he arrived in Rome, Bishop Magee dashed to the Papal apartment but on admission found that 'The embalmers were working on his body.'

He and the Polish secretary sat together for about an hour and a half. 'We shared and cried together over our experiences with him. And then he told me that about a fortnight previously he had been wheeling the Holy Father down the corridor from the dining room to the study. I know it well.'

Along that corridor, following the tradition of his predecessors, John Paul always stopped at a bronze bust of the Virgin Mary and on the day in question, while reaching from his wheelchair to touch it, 'he said to Monsignor Dziwisz, "We must not forget John!"

'"You have not forgotten him, Holy Father," the Monsignor replied. "You have left him many, many souvenirs."

'"I know I gave John many things. But I have something special I want to leave him. I want John to have this when I go."'

He swept both hands from his head to his knees. John Paul II wanted John Magee to have the white cassock and zucchetto (the white papal skullcap) he was wearing. Cleaned and carefully cocooned in a box by Roman nuns, the outfit is reverently stored in the Diocesan House at Cobh.

Faith, goodwill, hospitality, sharing, fervour, belonging, neighbourliness, helpfulness, generosity, co-operation, stamina, patience, celebration, loving and being loved in return – what more could we have wanted during that amazing Alleluia Weekend?

We should remind ourselves that this was not Ireland '79, The Rock Tour but a sacred event. Although in some ways it did feel as though we were entertaining a temporal superstar rather than an influential religious leader, the Irish people were acknowledging their faith in their supreme pastor. And when Bishop Magee looks back on the visit, he prays that 'we may never forget the message he left us: a call to fidelity, a call to peace, a call to love in Christ'.

We had a great time and we loved him, but on today's evidence, I don't think we all heard him. If we did, it went in one ear and out the other.

To finish on an irreverent note, I have to pass on my favourite Archbishop Marcinkus story.

After his Mass in the Phoenix Park, the Pope went into the hospitality tent for a few minutes' rest – and immediately waded into the food. Within minutes, above the hubbub of polite, respectful conversation around him, there rose the stentorian tones of the Archbishop: 'Hey! Get that guy away from the roast beef – he's due in the Nunciature in ten minutes . . .'

An Unmoving Statue

The Lonely Death of Ann Lovett

When John Paul II lifted off from Shannon, he left us two permanent memorials: the Celtic cross near Drogheda and the massive white cross that had graced the altar in the Phoenix Park. It is still visited by not only the faithful but by tourists and Dublin families on a day out.

Some images become iconic: the Sam Maguire cup held aloft; the mouth of a freckle-faced toddler smeared with ice cream on a sunny summer's day; a close-up of bare feet bleeding on the stony slopes of Croagh Patrick; flowers in waterlogged cellophane taped to a telegraph pole at the side of a rural road.

But it is those images that few of us have seen for ourselves that trouble us as citizens of Ireland: a newborn baby boy's body scored with twenty-eight wounds, washed up on a Kerry beach; the fatal battering dealt to Sophie Toscan du Plantier; the murder with

St Bernadette under the statue of Our Lady at the grotto where fifteen-year-old Ann Lovett and her baby boy died, 1979.

23

screwdrivers of two hard-working Polish men in a suburb of Dublin; the grotto dedicated to the Blessed Virgin in Granard, Co. Longford, where Ann Lovett and her baby son died with only each other and two impermeable statues for company.

Less than four and a half years after the population came joyfully together to celebrate Christianity in 1979, this girl and her baby died on cold ground under a drizzle. In some respects their deaths have come to illustrate everything that, until recent years, had remained hidden in Irish society.

We have some facts about the deaths of Ann Lovett and her tiny baby in that Marian shrine.

The baby weighed six and a half pounds.

He was male.

She lay on the ground to give birth.

It was drizzling.

It was cold.

It was lunchtime in her schoolyard not far away.

She was fifteen.

It is what we do not know that prompts imaginings at four o'clock in the morning. Did the baby cry? Thrash and flail? Or did he die quietly and without fuss? Did she hold him?

The story broke when someone in Granard could, in conscience, no longer bear the secrecy that surrounded the lonely death of Ann Lovett and her son. That person made a telephone call to the *Sunday Tribune* in Dublin. Emily O'Reilly wrote the piece and immediately after publication it was followed up by every media outlet in the country, including *The Gay Byrne Show*.

Gay is somewhat hesitant to talk about Ann Lovett now, largely because to him this was just one of hundreds of tragic incidents, events and phenomena his show covered during its long tenure. 'We heard of this child being found in a grotto and Kevin O'Connor was dispatched to find out what was going on.'

O'Connor was no stranger to big stories with sociological under- and overtones. For *The GB Show* he had reported on the case of Eileen Flynn, the teacher who was fired from her job in the south-east of the country because she had become pregnant 'out of wedlock'. (I've always been taken by that phrase, the idea that once you're wed you're locked. Head locked. Heart locked. Or, as Bessie Burgess has it in *The Plough and the Stars*, if in a different context: 'Yous are all nicely shanghaied now!')

Longford, with its lofty cathedral, was at the time a typical market town, redolent of paraffin, animal dung and the exhaust of tractors chuntering up and down the main street. When Kevin O'Connor arrived there, he found that due to the *Tribune* story, he was only one of a media pack, and that the local people had already drawn Granard and its secrets close around them. He got no hard information anywhere, and it was a group of ten- and eleven-year-olds who showed him the shrine where the fifteen-year-old and her baby son had died.

He discovered a teenage hangout, a small cottage in one of the town's streets, inside which were four or five 'undernourished' girls who, he felt, 'clearly knew what had happened'. He says he could also sense that the girls were not alone, that others were in the shadows, listening, as he tried without success to elicit information.

The nuns who had educated Ann Lovett and who must have known about her full-term pregnancy also refused to co-operate: their duty of confidentiality, said the sister-spokeswoman to one reporter who went to the convent to make enquiries, 'continues beyond the grave'.

But when he went to the cemetery, O'Connor says, 'There was somebody at her grave.'

The information that person divulged became the basis for his narrative for *The Gay Byrne Show*. He kept his informant's identity to himself, however, and has done so ever since. 'All I will say is that it was an adult and that person told me the entire story, including the use of rusty scissors to cut the umbilical cord.' He will not elaborate.

To outline this atmosphere, incidentally, is not to dump on Longford or rural Ireland. Although cracks were appearing and the light was getting in here and there, such closed environments were still endemic in Ireland. They are not even peculiar to this country. Movies set in many other nations show similar scenarios: how silence and secrecy can become the defensive – and attacking – weapons of choice; the common reaction is to pull up the drawbridge when the integrity of the community is threatened by outsiders.

'When Kevin came into studio that morning,' says Gay Byrne, 'he said to me, "Be careful what you ask me. Legally careful."' So O'Connor's report was run with little or no interjection. 'I remember thinking, even while he was speaking, What a wonderfully measured, slow, detailed account of his visit to Granard and what he saw and how he felt and what the reaction of the people of Granard was to him, which was hostile, bordering on aggressive.'

But the media maw is insatiable, as Gay knows very well, and when that particular report was finished, he put aside his brief for the item and switched mentally to the next story. 'I said, "Thank you, Kevin," and he went out.'

No one had any idea what was about to happen.

'The next thing was, we started getting letters. A deluge. From all over the country.' (Kevin O'Connor's recollection is that there was so much mail on the days immediately following his broadcast that the Post Office set aside special sacks.)

Gay had his first inkling of the size of the response when, a few days later after another programme, he returned to the office from his studio and found his team, with other staff, reading 'this extraordinary pile of letters. Those letters came from everywhere:

Main Street, Granard.

"I know bloody well what happened in Granard, because me too!" It was as if we had lifted a huge flat concrete flagstone, and underneath was crawling all this stuff. Incest and abuse and clerical abuse and so on.

'And my memory is that, next thing, Kevin said, "We're going to do a book."'

Ever the pragmatist, Byrne responded, 'Why a book? What advantage is that to us? They sent those letters to the programme. That's where they belong.' And so, for an entire programme, the letters were read by two actors, one male and one female. 'Considerably edited, of course, because most of them had included a lot of preliminary detail.' The decision to edit was to protect identities, to guard against libel actions and – he doesn't say this but let's be honest – for dramatic effect. They were read straight, in a serious but matter-of-fact tone.

The effect was devastating – and generated even more letters. 'I think,' Gay says now with considerable understatement, 'that was the start of the revelations about what was going on in Ireland. We always knew, but "we didn't know"; we always suspected but "we didn't suspect" . . .'

For Kevin O'Connor, the letters represented a mass breakout from purdah. It was as if each of those women had responded to a mysterious countrywide signal to break the formerly immutable rule 'Thou shalt hide.' 'It had been women's secret life,' he says.

From his own area in the south-west of the country he has personal knowledge of a woman in her thirties, a so-called 'domestic' who, in pre-contraception, pre-divorce, pre-right-to-travel Ireland, had strangled her 'illegitimate' baby. And some time after his Ann Lovett broadcast, during a visit to his home place, he met a doctor friend who, in place of the normal cordial greeting, looked quizzically at him: 'You'll have to stop doing reports like that. I'm called up into the hills around here every month to deal with the product of incest. I can't report it or the whole place will collapse.'

All these years later, he wonders if, perhaps, our new-fangled ethics of transparency, acceptance, broad-mindedness and balance could still be only skin deep, that it may be a mistake to take them for granted, and that the 'no' majority in the referendum on the Lisbon Treaty points to this.

Remember the Kerry Babies Tribunal? The one where Judge Kevin Lynch investigated the circumstances surrounding two dead babies, found miles apart and yet allegedly twins by different fathers born to a young girl called Joanne Hayes? Who, with the collusion of her family, allegedly killed them?

Although her own baby had died, the judge did not entertain the twins' fallacy in his report, and the second baby's origins, cause of death or parentage has never been definitively established. Over the six months of those proceedings, however, I heard many chilling things, including a piece of evidence that haunts me still. In his soft Kerry accent, a farmer in the witness box revealed that when he was ploughing a headland, it was not all that unusual to turn up a small skeleton. Kevin O'Connor heard something similar from his doctor friend: 'Put a bulldozer in anywhere . . .'

At least these things are less hidden (somewhat) now.

Ann Lovett frequently went home for lunch, but on 31 January 1984, it is not known whether her fellow pupils noticed her departure while they were eating their sandwiches and gossiping about the weekend.

She was a smoker. Although, again, it is not known how regularly she indulged, it has been reported that on her way to the grotto she called into a friend's house to borrow a cigarette. 'To borrow' may or may not be significant.

There were eleven people in her household.

Her school was co-educational, one of the first such in the country.

She was still conscious – although only barely – when she and her dead baby were found at four in the afternoon by a home-going schoolboy who had spotted her schoolbag lying on the ground.

A doctor was called, but it was too late to save her.

The grotto where Ann Lovett went to have her baby in secret was adjacent to the town's graveyard. Perhaps she thought she should bury him outside its wall. Well-founded though that surmise might be, since it was the custom and practice in our Christian country, it is only that: surmise. As, of course, is wondering whether Ann Lovett held her baby even briefly – or, with her own life ebbing as she lay beside him, if she was apologising to Our Lady, St Bernadette and Jesus for giving birth . . .

Did the blank eyes of the Virgin continue to stare into space over her head – or did Ann Lovett think that, for a split second, those eyes sparked towards her with forgiveness? Absolution? Compassion, even?

So there you are. That's what most of us – including Gay Byrne and Kevin O'Connor – know, imagine and hypothesise about the short life of Ann Lovett and her little son.

The Master

Your Host – Gay Byrne!

After a frightening start, things improved for another mother who appeared on *The Late Late Show* to beg help for her baby son, a chubby, dark-haired heartbreaker with big brown eyes, so that he would not die for lack of a liver transplant.

He's studying communications in DIT now – thanks, says Gay Byrne, to 'the most amazing and incredible outpouring of goodwill on the part of the Irish people, who did the most amazing things – the kind of things that since became part and parcel of the Telethon: bed pushes, golf classics, rebuilding sheds, two-shillings-a-mile runs and so forth.' The even better news is that the Colin McStay Fund was so heavily oversubscribed that there is still money there at the

Crumlin Children's Hospital to finance research on the specific liver problems that threatened him.

In his heyday, Gay Byrne was central to a host of 'days we remember', although he continues to protest that he was just doing his job and that changing society had never been his goal. Whether he accepts it or not, he was pivotal to the process of levering open what had been the most tightly shuttered and darkest rooms in the Irish psyche. Remember the strand on radio where mothers confessed to not liking one of their children? Remember the shock he gave us all when he displayed a condom on *The Late Late Show*, and showed us how it worked, right on our own television screens by our own firesides? Remember the appearances of Madame Sin (Cynthia Payne) and the Lesbian Nuns? Nuala O'Faoláin's multiple revelations?

On radio, remember the Silence? 'Years and years and years of "ask your mother to pass the salt" in houses all over the country? It was a regular thing. William Trevor has written about this, as has McGahern, and when I was growing up on the South Circular Road there were houses where the Silence prevailed and everybody knew. It was just accepted that this was the way it was in those houses.'

But 'your host' begs you to recall not just the Ann Lovetts and loneliness but the fun, laughter and entertainment as well; the peregrinations of Joe Duffy as the out-and-about reporter: 'He convulsed me one morning when we sent him to interview Prince Charles who was visiting the Mansion House and, of course, Joe couldn't get further than the barrier. Through the general noise, we could hear him, with this posh voice he was putting on because he was talking to royalty: "Excuse me, Your Royal Highness, excuse me? *Gay Byrne Show*, could we have a word? Royal Highness? Royal Highness? Excuse me? Hello?"'

On TV there were the speciality acts, singers and musicians, choirs, circus artists and bands – including the launch of what seemed like the

Previous: Gaybo's Harley – U2's thank you gift, his last Late Late Show, *1999.*

Opposite top: Colin McStay, pictured with his parents Leonard and Margaret, at Dublin Airport on his way to the USA to await a liver transplant.

Opposite bottom: A slick debut – not! Boyzone, Late Late Show, *1993*

Band Most Likely to Sink Without Trace and that turned into Boyzone.

Gay just loved comedians: Billy Connolly, Tom O'Connor – 'He still sends me a Christmas card every year', the home-grown Brendan O'Carroll, d'Unbelievables and the controversial Tommy Tiernan: 'Comedians generally are suffering souls but he's a very serious, very

thoughtful guy. Amazing innate charm, with the dimple and the smile and the lovely teeth. We had him on a couple of times and he got funnier and funnier and never put a foot wrong.'

Until the sketch about Christ's Crucifixion, generally considered blasphemous. It still galls Byrne to remember it: he regards it as having been a 'profound blunder' by the programme.

Outside broadcast:
d'Unbelievables
with Pat Shortt and
Jon Kenny, GB
show, 1998.

The gag had been vetted, if not by the host himself during Tiernan's show in the Olympia Theatre, but at midnight before a young and beer-fuelled crowd and far from the folks who tuned in on TV to see what Gay was up to.

Where pure gags are concerned, Gay Byrne has a high regard for Frank Carson's delivery and timing: 'Annie Murphy sits up in bed: "I didn't know you were a bishop!"

'"When did you ever see a plumber wearing a hat like this?"'

Gay liked Annie Murphy. The interview with her was broadcast in connection with the publicising of her book, *Forbidden Fruit*. Do you remember how Annie compared her joy at sharing a love affair and a son with the Bishop of Galway to flying 'on gossamer wings'? Says Gay, 'She was attractive. She was smart and sexy and very intelligent and so on,' but he got into trouble with that one too. 'I got a ferocious drubbing afterwards.'

The problem arose towards the end of the interview. 'I said something along the lines of "If he's half the man his father was . . ." [of the son, Peter] in response to which, seeming to slap him down, she replied, "I didn't do too badly myself," and abruptly finished the interview. The studio audience gasped, and the *Irish Times* reviewer subsequently asserted that Annie Murphy had been subjected to a pre-arranged 'ambush' by a 'mini-mob' in the front row of the audience.

This still stings. He says that the four-woman 'mini-mob' had been named in Annie's book and were there by invitation, with the prior consent of both Annie and her lawyer. And, he says, 'I could have been smart at the time and put in a panel and let them do the dirty work, but I insisted on doing the interview myself.' And he had felt, since her book gave her own view of events, it was incumbent on him, in fairness, to represent the bishop.

Not that he approved of Casey's actions: 'Eamonn Casey did three things wrong. When he was made Bishop of Galway, I think he should

Annie Murphy, 1993.

have taken the opportunity to say, "Look, fellas, before you make me a bishop, I need to tell youse something. Woman. Son. Dah-di-dah-di-dah." I like to think that, even then, most Irish people would have said, "OK! Whoever is without sin . . . It could have happened to a bishop . . ." And so on.'

'He didn't do that, he denied his son, he dipped into the funds. And then he ran. That was all unforgivable.'

He believes that this was a time when, in Ireland generally, there was an upsurge of 'ferocious' anti-Church sentiment, which added to the public sense that Annie Murphy was 'whiter than white and the bishop was blacker than black. Anything that could be seen as being said against her was viewed as a terrible mortal sin, and anything said in favour of him was treachery. And I think I got caught in the middle of that.'

After the show, he approached his interviewee to ascertain how upset she was; '"I'm sorry you feel that I was unfair."

'And she said, "No, no, it was just that I thought that the entire audience was against me."'

Gay, relieved, rushed to reassure her: '"If I'm any judge of audiences after all these years, they were completely on your side." She accepted that. And then she and her lawyer and Cróna [Gay's daughter, who was working in the hospitality area of *The Late Late Show* at the time] went off to Lillie's or wherever they went.'

There were many controversies during the long run of Gay's television and radio shows, many, many 'comings-out' about affairs, alcoholism, sexual orientation, drug-taking, brutality, suffering and just plain ignorance. Although *Liveline* has perfected the art, it was not the begetter of confessional broadcasting in Ireland. Joe Duffy learned at the feet of a master.

Do you remember 21 March 1980? A single event dwarfed the Iran hostage crisis. It superseded television coverage of the presidential battle between Jimmy Carter and Ronald Reagan and took that contest off the cover of Time *magazine . . .*

I'll give you a clue: it happened in Texas. It concerned a bullet that ricocheted around the world . . .

Yeah. JR was shot. Half the population of Great Britain and, it seems to me, the entire population of Ireland tuned in to watch it happen.

But do you remember who shot him? Sue Ellen? Bobby? Cliff? Miss Ellie? (Hardly.) The poisoned dwarf?

Do you remember we all wore 'I Shot JR' T-shirts (and I see that one of the characters in Killinaskully wears his still)?

Yeah, but who shot him, really? This was to be revealed during the fourth episode of the third series, to be broadcast on 21 November. The bookies geared up for a last-minute rush and we all forgot that the twenty-second was the anniversary of someone else having been shot in Dallas, but not in a mansion – from a grassy knoll. There was feck-all in the newspapers about that, and we didn't care anyways, as we stocked up on the popcorn and the Taytos.

An attorney made an astounding offer to anyone who was interested: for a large fee, he would fly eastwards on your behalf,

The Ewings at Southfork, 1979. Bobby, Pamela Miss Ellie, J.R. Lucy, Jock and Sue Ellen.

somewhere far beyond any relevant US timeline, watch Dallas, and when he had discovered who shot JR, he would telephone you so you could place your bet.

So, yeah, there is always one.

And, by the way, it was Kristin. The sister-in-law.

These Are the Dreams of the Common People

What Did You Do with Your SSIA, Daddy?

Free money from the government? Nothing like it anywhere else in the world. Your cousin in Darwin was green with envy. Your kid sister, 'illegal' in San Francisco, was pissed off because, being non-resident, she couldn't get in on the act.

That's not to say she hadn't had a go. In her name, the second sister had put a few bob into the Irish bank account kept open for sentimental reasons – and had scrawled a spidery signature on the SSIA form, giving the mammy's address. The mammy, though, had got to hear about this and wouldn't have it. She had a sister a bishop.

Kid sister apart, 1,170,208 people signed up for the scheme and when the government's 'free money' was added to their savings, the sum accumulated was eighteen billion. That, ladies and gentlemen, is eighteen and nine noughts or, putting it another way, 18,000,000,000. Thanks to Charlie McCreevy, Ireland Inc was basking in a warm sea of expectation.

To its creator, the SSIA booty wasn't free money but tax forgone. Those to whom this was clear from the start should skip the next few lines. For the rest of us, the point is that if you were a tax payer, the money you put into your SSIA was from your earned, already-tax-paid, net income. So when the government added to your stash every month, all it was doing was giving you a refund. And to make things fair, for people on social welfare benefit, the state paid you the sum you would have paid on what you were saving, had it been from an earned and taxed income. You put in ten quid from your benefit, the government added two quid fifty.

'I think technically you could class it as a negative income tax – at least that was the principle behind it.' Charlie is in Dublin for some class of a lunch meeting. He flew in this morning and had agreed to make time to meet me.

I had been pathetically early as usual, early enough to be seated – and trying to be invisible – in the front office of the European Commission Office on the corner of Molesworth Street and Dawson Street in Dublin when the Commissioner himself breezed in. Early enough to hear that he was greeted by the uniformed front-of-house attendant with a cheery 'Hello, Charlie.' He might be M'sieur le Commissioner in Brussels, but here we know it's far from pâté he was reared.

Killeenmore, Sallins, Co. Kildare.

He was eating a packet sandwich and drinking a cup of tea when I was shown into his office. Brussels hasn't had much of an effect on his demeanour and posture – no velvety handshake, no deep and sincere smile of welcome – and as for the suit, it's a Good Suit but not a Great Suit and definitely Fianna Fáil.

The surroundings are pleasant, if functional, but with Mr McCreevy there, we could as well be meeting at a weekday mart. I mean that nicely. 'You haven't changed a bit' is a common compliment in Ireland and, in the Commissioner's case, it's true and to his credit: on the surface anyhow, he wears high office as lightly as if it's not there at all.

That's not to say that the eyes miss a thing.

He produces what looks like an envelope but could be a bit of a jotter (I'm not making this up) covered with handwriting. 'I made a few notes on the plane on the way over. You think you remember all these things but you don't – so fire away! Ask me what you like.'

We fire away. SSIAs, Mr McCreevy?

'We got off to a great start in 2001, but there were a lot of myths about it. The first was, some of the commentators had it that "He's doing this to cool inflation." The answer to that is "Bollocks!" Excuse the expression.'

It's not really an apology. He had paused for effect.

'Inflation was a bit high at the time and there's a theory that to cool it you have to take money out of the economy, et cetera, but I don't subscribe to that theory for the Irish economy. The main purpose was to encourage people to save. People weren't saving, barring paying off their mortgage, which is a form of saving, and the bit of life insurance, I suppose. At the time we had building societies and banks and different groups who were putting forward ideas about savings but they all had vested interests. The actual idea about it was totally my own. It had struck me that with all the success we'd had in the previous years, simple things like putting the few bob aside for the rainy day had been forgotten about. People were spending like there was no tomorrow.'

Dear God, don't remind me, Charlie. Wasn't Ireland a great place to live, though – and was that only a few years ago? When 'the

IFSC, Customs Docks, Dublin.

bounty', as they call it in North Kerry, that healing and nutritious syrup from Europe, was flowing; when we were whitening our teeth and sporting year-round tans because of the quarterly mini-breaks we could afford thanks to Michael O'Leary. The IFSC and associated buildings had spread like a rose-tinted rash over the

Dublin docklands, cranes were playing noughts and crosses on the Dublin skyline and waving at the exiles flying home overhead to take up good jobs. While in Tidy Towns and Specially Commended Villages all over the country, the tall skinny latte had overtaken the pint of plain.

We had *Riverdance* and Jack Charlton and Sonia O'Sullivan; we had Gucci and Jo Malone in BTs where there were fights over Fendi handbags. We went to chariddy lunches and erected marquees to hold weddings costing more than the GDP of Ethiopia. It was a kind of paradise, if we'd only realised it. And if the weather had been a bit better, of course, and if we hadn't had to read stuff in the papers about clerical sexual abuse and drugs and gun crime and 'consistent poverty' . . .

To put the cap on it, along came Charlie with his Big Idea.

At this point I have to disclose that the transcription of this interview was a nightmare. 'Charlie McCreevy enthusiastic' is 'Garret FitzGerald enthusiastic' squared. So, Commissioner, you'll have to forgive me if I've missed out, misrepresented or mangled you. Blame Sony. No half-speed.

So. Was there a eureka moment?

Did I mention that the Commissioner is a discursive thinker? The SSIA is the destination. There's a path to be followed.

'I always wanted to be Minister for Finance but I never thought I was going to be anything at any stage in my career. I never thought I'd end up a minister for anything. Fourteen years and eight months on the back benches under Mr Haughey and everything else, and I understood that, and Mr Haughey and I ended up as quite good friends, started off as good friends, had our difficult moments, but I always kept up a good relationship with him and I always understood why he couldn't promote me – the rest of the party would have gone mad because I'd been against him and all that, and then Albert [Reynolds] came along and I was promoted.'

He mentions his fourteen years and eight months in the back-bench gulag quite often.

'At various stages during the fourteen years and eight months on the back benches I was going to give it up altogether – I just got fed up with it, a whole lot of reasons, to do with my marriage as well, to be perfectly frank about it. That was '84 and '85 but then I got a new lease of life and I enjoyed every role I had in politics.'

One of those roles was giving interviews as spokesman – read, 'loose cannon' – on anything that occurred to the interviewer or to himself. 'I was regarded as an independent voice. I had views about this, that and the other, so people had me on their programmes. I enjoyed all that. I commented on everything.

'Then I became minister under Albert.'

Did he ask for it?

He reacts with horror. 'Oh, God, no! No – no! I never asked anybody for anything ever. Never asked Albert or Bertie or anybody for anything, ever, on any occasion. Never.'

Guess he never asked.

He must have let it be known, though, that he was available? Like, fourteen years and eight months on the back benches . . .

'No! Never. Never.'

On taking office, Albert Reynolds shuffled – and shuffled off – his deck of cabinet ministers with the ruthlessness of a football manager during a transfer window. Two of the beneficiaries were a pair of rural TDs who occupied the same office in Leinster House and had become fast friends – 'two people who'd never been junior ministers or anything. Myself and Brian Cowen.'

The Commissioner is proud of the company he kept and of that promotion. 'We were the only two who went straight from the back benches, no junior ministers, no nothing. He just thought we were good.'

At first he had to bide his time: the promotion in February 1992 was to Social Welfare. Then from 1993 to 1994, he served time in Tourism and Trade – and then Fianna Fáil was dumped into opposition. At long last he was given the opportunity to get his teeth into the Finance portfolio, if only as a shadow.

By the way, he wouldn't have minded being Taoiseach, 'if it didn't mean leading the Fianna Fáil party. I could be Taoiseach all right, I'd make a good Taoiseach, but I don't have the skills for leading Fianna Fáil. Even though I come from a Fianna Fáil background and I understand the Fianna Fáil way. They're a very diverse group of people.'

Before I can interject to ask him to expound on this (the tape shows

Budget day, 2 December 1998: Charlie McCreevy outside Government Buildings.

I tried really hard), he's away down the path ahead of us both and I have to keep up or I'll lose him altogether.

When his party came back into office in 1997, Charlie McCreevy was given his head by Bertie Ahern. He came to the Ministry of Finance 'with very clear and set ideas. And, lucky enough, I had a Taoiseach who allowed me – I don't think if I was him, if I was in Bertie's shoes, I'd have allowed someone like me to do what I did.'

His two core principles during his time in Finance were: 'for a thing to work well it has to be simple and straightforward' and 'do a few major things well, rather than do a whole lot of things and do them badly'.

What happens, he says, not only in Ireland but in executives throughout the world, is that 'Someone has an idea about a scheme, and then everyone thinks too much about the minuses and the loopholes.'

Loopholes, shmoopholes. 'If I'd gone out and done impact assessments and consultations and all that kind of thing, the SSIA scheme never would have got off the ground. You'd get all this negative stuff, you'd get columnists writing reports . . . I'm a little bit of a subscriber to the American approach as opposed to the European approach. In Europe you have to get the commas, the colons, the full stops all perfect; it takes years to consider it. Somebody described the Euro approach as "Get ready, aim, fire!"

'The American approach is "Fire! And then we'll see the mistakes afterwards and we'll correct them . . ."

'It's not the job of the civil service to come up with these ideas, their job is to protect the public purse and to point out the downfalls, but what you have to do if you're in a government party is not to let a good idea be ballsed-up by the system.'

By the way, he has 'nothing but good' to say about the Department of Finance, and his 'positive' experiences there. 'It's the most outstanding department of state in my view, but I never expected that I'd go in one day and someone would walk into the office and say, "Here's a very brilliant idea, Minister McCreevy – you should do this!" That's not going to happen. They'll analyse the thing for you, they'll give you the pluses if there are any, they'll give you millions and millions of negatives . . . But when I said, "I'm going to do some things my way and that's it", those fellas in Finance, they followed the lead. Not like trying to go round you, which is what they do in other departments with other ministers. I said, "We're doing something." We did it.'

While the minister was cutting his teeth, he spent quite some time meditating on the behaviour of the newly profligate and hedonistic population, who now seemed to care not a *thraneen* for the future. How to get everyone back into the old-fashioned habit of saving?

Incentives.

Plus something to do with people feeling that they were getting away with not paying tax. When he was running his accountancy business, he had noticed that in the month of March, there was always a flood of clients coming in, with borrowed money, to invest in John Bruton's Business Expansion Scheme so they could get tax back. To add to his belief in incentives, he has an intuitive feel for the passionate Irish hatred of giving money to the government. The germ of a plan was beginning to grow legs in the Petri dish that was the minister's desk.

One of those germs reproachfully carried the reason why another pet project, the PRSA (Personal Retirement Savings Account) scheme had been so slow to take off. On paper a generous and tax-efficient method of paying into a personal private pension fund, its uptake had been disappointing to say the least. The reason, Charlie thinks, was that the financial institutions didn't push the scheme. In their view, he believes, the bureaucracy attached to it was more trouble than it was worth. There wasn't enough in it for them.

This realisation led to the eureka moment. 'You've got to give incentives to both sides. Over the years there'd been various ideas, post-office schemes, bonds and so on ['bonnnds' – it's clear he doesn't get much of a kick out of 'bonnnds'] but the eureka thing in this is very simple. Win-win. Tax breaks for the people. Incentives for the banks.

'A guy in Revenue' came up with an enhancement of the basics of the minister's putative scheme. The 'refund' should be structured on a monthly basis.

That was the genius moment. The too-good-to-be-true thing became true when actual money became tangible. Punters would see it going into their accounts every month and wouldn't have to wait for the Never-Never Land of the future. 'I didn't allow any convoluted stuff, letting it get messed up with a whole lot of caveats.'

The carrot for savers was obvious. But since the scheme had been created to establish the habit of regular saving, the minister added a stick: you had to stay with the scheme for the full five years you'd signed up for. If you withdrew the money, every penny, your principal, the interest it had earned and the 'free' money the state added was all taxed at 23 per cent.

'I was told, "Oh, that's very severe, Minister."

'"I don't care. It'll keep people in."'

And not wishing to decimate the Exchequer, the minister put a maximum of £200 (€253) on the figure that could be saved. 'I doubt if Dermot Desmond or Albert was in the scheme, although I don't know! You'd never know!' So it was a personal invitation to every John and Judy Doe in the country to think about what they were doing with their money.

The financial institutions were delighted: '"Jeez, we'll get more customers and cash flow."' The seller has to know he's getting something out of it as well. That's well recognised in business, whereas civil servants don't appreciate that at all!' The Exchequer wouldn't lose everything because the interest given by the financial institutions was taxable at 23 per cent and would roll in as people started encashing, during 2006 and 2007. 'There was something there for all of us.'

Once they understood what was on offer, the institutions jumped. 'Everybody started competing for the business. I went to Longford one day and a branch there had installed cardboard cut-outs of me in the branch to sell it!'

Even the commentators got in on the sales drive: 'You had Eddie Hobbs telling people they'd be crazy not to get in on it – and in the last months [during the set-up period] George Lee was one of the best salesmen I had! He was on the radio, going, "You'd be mad not to do this – this is the sale of the century."'

There were many who tried to find the catches or, more particularly, the ulterior motives. Politicians always have ulterior motives, right? Hidden agendas? Objectives of personal aggrandisement or – hey! Here's one! – election gains?

'One of the funnier things concerned elections. At the start, all the commentators said the scheme was nonsense. Then, as people started piling into it, they said, "He's done this to win the next election for Fianna Fáil."

'Very interesting that: such brilliant foresight. Remember, I gave a year to join, to start on the first of May 2001 and to end on the thirtieth of April 2002. At that stage we wouldn't have had the 2002 election and, anyway, since 1969 no same administration had been re-elected . . .

'And was I so brilliant I was able to get the election fixed in 2002? And so really brilliant that I was able to sort out the following one in 2007 as well? It's a lovely story and I'd like to believe it, but that's not true.'

Then there was the other myth: when this is done, they'll draw it all out and they'll spend like mad. 'These were the ridiculous questions in the first few years. "What'll happen to the economy, Minister, if people spend it all?"

'"They won't."

'"But surveys say they will."

'"I don't believe those surveys."

'Surveys kept being produced during the thing and I kept saying, "I don't believe a word of it. You're expecting me to believe that the Irish people are that mad? They're not." I was playing a hunch. It's a fundamental McCreevy principle that the Irish people are far more intelligent than the people they elect and definitely far more intelligent than the people that write this kind of stuff. I said, "I think people will continue to save," and I kept saying it. I also said, "It's the people's money. If they want to spend it in Shelbourne Park, in the Curragh, if they want to fly to Barbados – this is giving back their own money. And while I don't think they'll all race off to spend their money in Las Vegas, they can do what they like and we're not going to penalise the ninety per cent for the doings of the ten." I've been proven right.'

He has. According to one Survey, 83 per cent of people have continued to save.

Charlie absolutely loves the notion of 'ordinary' people having, probably for the first time in their lives, 'that kind of a lump sum of money sitting there all for themselves. It's a feeling. It gives people a certain amount of confidence.' He continues to receive postcards 'from faraway places like Lanzarote, thanking me for their holidays; I get Mass bouquets from old people'. And at Punchestown Races in 2008, long past the ending of the scheme, he was a guest in one of the corporate boxes. One of the waitresses took him aside: '"I never got to thank you, Mr McCreevy, for my SSIA. Myself and my two children saved the max all together, and we put the whole lot together

at the end and we bought a place in Spain. We go out there every few weeks. Lovely place. We'd never have it without you."'

It gave him 'a bit of a thrill' to hear it: 'You always get a bit of a thrill when one of your hunches, your children, turns out well. I know the ordinary people it affected – I grew up with them.'

Growing up in Kildare has gelled his underlying philosophy not

With thanks to Charlie: Pat, Kate, David and Noel Murphy on their holiday of a lifetime at the Grand Canyon, Summer 2007.

51

only of politics, but of life. Most of the farms around Killeenmore, having been distributed by the Land Commission, were small, usually of around twenty acres. One of the exceptions belonged to a family called Kilgallon and everyone for miles around was on watch when Paddy Kilgallon, installed a milking machine, the first in the district. It wasn't long before others had one too. And even before the milking machines, a steady stream of people was emulating the first man to put in a well linked to a scullery with a sink and a tap. 'Three years – everyone had done it. It's always stayed with me. People copy.'

The urge to copy can be negative as well as positive. 'I remember in the eighties and nineties where you'd canvass a housing estate and nobody was working. And in fact, if anybody went working they'd be in trouble because everybody else would be against them. There wasn't a lot of work, although there was some, but the problem was there wasn't a lot of difference financially between working and not working.

'And I can understand that. You'd go out maybe on a Sunday night and the alarm goes off at maybe half six the next morning, and it's wet and miserable outside and sure it's only going to work and getting hassle, instead of staying in your nice comfortable bed and getting a bit of dole. My theory when I got to Finance was that the gap should be made wider. Give working people back a bit of tax and give an incentive to people to get out of the bed.

'And the other people see it and say, 'Look at that, there's one of the Purcell lads going to work and he's getting on . . .'

This theory inevitably led to swords crossed with organisations such as CORI and its leaders, particularly Father Seán Healy. 'I'm afraid there was no love lost between him and myself.' And the former minister unrepentantly dismisses critics who, from the start, rubbished his scheme as just another manifestation of the much-quoted gap between the haves and the have-nots. 'This was for everyone. The minimum you could pay was ten pounds a month. That's two pounds fifty a week. Sure you wouldn't get a packet of fags for that – and I used to be a smoker.'

And things did improve. In canvassing those same estates between 1997, when he took up the ministry, and the election of 2002, 'you'd be looking in the front doors and they all had wooden floors . . .'

He worries about the Irish national disease of begrudgery. 'It'll take maybe fifty years – from maybe 2000 – that we'll get used to people with wealth. When you and I were growing up, the biggest thing in Ireland was sex. You couldn't talk about it, or do it, or think about it. Mass every Sunday, no sex before marriage, and if you did it you were gone.

'Nowadays, Irish people don't care about the sexual behaviour of politicians. The British are fascinated about the sexual lives of celebrities and politicians, always the front page. Ireland? That's gone. The Catholic Church has no say in it any more. And that's welcome. The only sin in Ireland now is having money.

'It's an extraordinary thing. The media in this country have specialised in begrudgery. You don't find that in London because they've had hundreds and hundreds of years of wealthy people and landed gentry and so on; it's even admired. Here, you could have six affairs a day and still stay a public figure, but if you were a wealthy businessman . . . As far as the media is concerned, the sin is having the wealth.

'When we were growing up in Kildare, the McCreevys had this, the Cruises had that, the Millses had that, the Humphreys had that. We all knew the GP had such and such, we all knew that someone had a son went into a grand job in the civil service, someone got a job as a Guard, and we all said, "Well, that was always a decent family."

'That's all gone. Primarily sponsored by some of the newspapers in this country, there's this begrudgery instead of celebrating the business people we have who've made a bit of money and who, most of them, employ thousands and thousands of people. Some of them live in the country, some of them live outside the country, but they're spending more money in this country than anybody else. That should be celebrated. You want people to spend, you want people to come here and live and make it attractive.

'But we were so long downtrodden, if anyone did well and then fell a bit, "Sure the Purcells were never any good. The great-grandfather there stole sheep or sold the wrong horse at a fair in Naas one day, a horse that was supposed to have four good legs and when we got the horse home he had only two good legs . . ."

So: 2050 before Irish people will be comfortable with neighbours' success? 'Right now, it's still going back to the land, downtrodden, and being occupied, and isn't the oul' weather terrible, always dust and darkness . . .'

He met Denis O'Brien at a social function, just after the businessman had offered the FAI a large sum of money to help with the finding of a new soccer manager for the Republic's team. 'It was of no benefit to him to help the Irish soccer team, and I said, "Denis, why in the name of God would you do that? They'll eat you."

Eat him we did, as we ate Noel Smyth who, in order to alleviate the crisis in Dublin hospitals, had the temerity to offer to build a hospital, free. What's the agenda, Joe? No effin' capitalist ever does nothin', Joe, without there bein' an agenda . . . What's he gettin' owa it?

Then there's J. P. McManus, who was given the 2007 award as National Philanthropist of the Year by the Community Foundation. 'He's the biggest philanthropist in the country. He gave fifty million for a stadium that we never used and we had to give the money back. He gave thirty million for educational scholarships. But there were a whole lot of negative letters about him on this too. I was going to say I just don't understand it. The unfortunate thing is that I do understand it.'

In America, by contrast, 'You're sweeping the street but you manage to buy your own house and it's "Good man, Charlie!" You do better for yourself and you manage to buy a house in Florida and employ a bunch of other sweepers and it's "Better man, Charlie!"'

As an aside, Charlie is sick of all this Openness, Transparency and Accountability malarkey. 'I call it the Goddess OTA . . . In Europe, you needn't be afraid to talk to a person. You're encouraged the whole time to talk to every type of person, every type of organisation, banks, insurance companies and everything – because how else would you know what they want or need, or what you want or need unless you talk to everybody?

'Here they think it's all right to meet trade unions but you're not supposed to talk to businessmen or wealthy people, even if they're employing thousands. You certainly shouldn't be seen with them. I don't subscribe to that.'

Economically, it's far chillier, these days, but the wise virgins out there will still have the wherewithal to buy blankets. As for the foolish ones, didn't we have a great time? The breast enhancements, dental work, college courses, little run-arounds, extensions, new kitchens and leather suites, wooden floors, hideaways in Connemara and all that meeting each other in the Maldives or Cairns, as we criss-crossed the globe, taking 'holidays of a lifetime'.

Such mental resources for the winters ahead as we extract the rusting Super Ser from the shed, find a cobbler's last in a junk shop, and again take up that knitting we abandoned long ago.

Wasn't it great?

Yes, We Can! Yes, We Can! Yes! Yes! Yes!

Birth of a Phenomenon
– *Riverdance*

Great . . . great . . . great . . . Did you see it on the telly? Or (oh, magic!) were you actually there in the Point Theatre on 30 April, 1994?

I was wearing my 'good' outfit to fit in with the ritzy audience around me. I heard the ethereal voices of Anúna. I heard Bill Whelan's atmospheric, all-enveloping music. I saw the long, graceful limbs of Jean Butler covering the huge stage as though they were barely touching it.

Before we took our seats that night, we had met someone we knew in the lobby of the Point: she was working on the show and had seen the dress rehearsal. 'Whatever you do,' she said, looking at my husband meaningfully, 'don't leave during the interval act.' Kevin was a smoker then.

She was probably right, I thought, as I admired Jean Butler's supple arms and legs, the way her gorgeous costume fitted her like a second skin. Probably. But it had been a long evening so far, and the voting was still to come. It was a bit warm. This was lovely but I could do with a bit of fresh air . . .

Then I heard a sudden change of tempo. Drums beating competitively. Something was going to happen—

WHAM! It sure did. Those clothes seemed to lift off my back as, Nijinsky-like, Michael Flatley, blond tresses streaming over a violet blouse and tight trousers, exploded horizontally from the wings. For the next five minutes or so, I don't think I breathed. I must have, but if I did it was in gasps.

'I knew, from the moment I heard the music, that we had something extraordinary on our hands.' This is the voice of Moya Doherty, mother of *Riverdance*, progenitor of the thirty-ninth Eurovision Song Contest extravaganza LIVE from the Point.

In latter years, especially since *Riverdance* expanded to become a theatrical show and a travelling worldwide phenomenon, the interval act has become almost as competitive as the contest itself. Moya's, though, was the mother lode and for instant hair-raising impact, no country has matched it since.

Let's reel backwards a little – no pun intended. Because this was Ireland, pre-contest, whatever was going on down there in the dance rehearsal rooms came to the attention of the flame-keepers and guardians of Our Culture who were outraged. This showbiz thing was engaged in subverting the purity of the slip jig, three-hand reel and hornpipe. If it was allowed to continue, it would destroy our tradition, hard wrested from the coloniser's tight grasp and fought for by our forebears. It was obviously cheap thrills at the expense of core values.

Previous:
Riverdance is born.
Eurovision Song
Contest, The Point,
Dublin, 1994.

Opposite:
Jean Butler and
Michael Flatley in
rehearsal.

Dear Director General –
I have been told –

Dear Mr Barry –
I am extremely concerned . . .

Dear Sir,
I am disgusted. I don't pay my licence fee in order to . . .

Alongside the fundamental complaints of tackiness and treason was the one about the betrayal involved in casting Irish-Americans in lead roles.

RTÉ remained steadfast – mostly –but how did Ms Doherty herself react to such pre-emptive criticism? 'I grew up with it. I had a highly critical mother. I'm stubborn and tenacious and if I think something is right and I want to do it I'll find a way to do it. From a work perspective, I do listen to people – but if I feel in my heart that something is right . . .' She smiles. 'As you know, Irish dancing is very political.'

'Personally,' she adds, 'I'm not a bit thick-skinned. Not many women are.'

She heard the final mix of Whelan's music for the first time just before the 'madness' started for her production team, the twenty-hour days, round-the-clock phone calls and meetings. As executive producer of RTÉ's live spectacular, Doherty hired a minibus to take her 'small, tight' group for dinner. 'I can't remember exactly where we went, it was a thank-you to them personally from me for work done – and a good-luck for what was to come.' She had brought the music recording with her and on the way down 'I said to them, "We've got to listen to this!"'

It put them all in the mood for a great dinner. And on the way back – 'and of course we were all slightly sozzled' – she played it for them over and over again. 'I was going, "And this is where Flatley enters," and "This is where the line of dancers come in from each side," and we were all roaring.'

Just like the huge crowd in the Point on the night itself when the drums, having jousted with the hammering feet of that final long, long line of dancers and the last sexy twirling of Butler and Flatley, pounded to a triumphant, soaring crescendo and stopped.

Just like the hundreds of blasé, jaded, seen-it-all-before guests, who jumped to their feet, throwing their toned, bedizened arms in the air to join with the cheers of thousands of 'ordinary' punters.

Just like the sophisticated mandarins of the European Broadcasting Union, including Jean-Bernard Münch, the organisation's powerful Secretary General, who parked his nicotine-substitute gum in his cheek so he could engage in the visceral, almost primal group reaction. (This might seem fanciful: how can she know that? That has to be invention and embroidery. I know it because the man was sitting beside me.)

'I knew from the beginning that this was really powerful. And different.' Ms Doherty smiles again. 'We were going to be proud of it.'

She is slim, dressed in black, with very high wedge-heeled black shoes and a minimum of jewellery. Her posture, even while sitting, is upright yet graceful, like a ballet dancer in repose. On each anniversary of that night, which proved subsequently to change her own life and that of her family, she always remembers it – just for herself. Makes no big deal about it. 'I mark it quietly in my head.' In latter years, however, the date has become 'a little skewed,' woven into the memory of her father's death, on 29 April 2000, the day before the show's eighth birthday.

Although her name is a household one, frequently linked in the press with that of her husband and business partner John McColgan,

Moya Doherty with husband John McColgan.

as 'the Golden Couple', she is a very private person. 'I made a conscious and deliberate decision not to be defined.'

For instance, she doesn't rate her listing as a 'serial entrepreneur' in one of those 'Women in Business' lists run occasionally during newspaper silly seasons. 'I don't do press stuff. Years ago I stopped. I don't turn up at opening nights. I do go to the odd one, but it's a conscious decision. Those things aren't important to me. That kind of thing is important to some people – they've got an ease or a joyousness of personality and they love it. I don't.'

Her personality is welcoming, friendly and generous, and throughout this interview, she names and gives credit to others for the success she has enjoyed. Yet she is hung about with a combination of reserve and a sort of measured alertness. She had agreed readily to be interviewed and had laid down no advance parameters but she hadn't needed to. Because of the depth of tone with which she speaks when she introduces the subject of her father's passing, I can see it is not appropriate to pursue her.

This year she remembered the *Riverdance* anniversary late on the day: 'I couldn't believe it had been fourteen years. Mark was four, Danny was two, there was no Ross – he's our youngest. Extraordinary. It seems like yesterday and yet it seems like a lifetime ago.' She marked it by texting her sister.

The business, some might say art, of the producer is not just to envisage projects, or even to set and manage budgets, but to bring creatives together and set up the framework and context in which they can work in harmony, a team in which each is at peak ability. When Moya Doherty was handed such a plum assignment – and massive budget – this was exactly what she did.

In the public mind she is now associated only with the *Riverdance* element of that Eurovision show and we probably forget that each contest is actually an enormous, live gala, involving the management of not only hundreds of components but thousands of people, right down to specific squads for accreditation, airport greeting, fixing-it, desk-manning and hospitality. Someone has to be in charge of laminated name badges, complete with safety pins, for each member of the big foreign delegations and accompanying media. The souvenir pens, press packs and disposable coffee cups have to be designed and manufactured.

You have technological, creative and filming challenges so that the introductions to each song will sell your country. There are the catering challenges, the arrangement of suitable entertainment for the delegations (and the quaintly named 'accompanying persons') who will be in Ireland for longer than just the night of the contest, the venue, set, lighting, sound and camera challenges, the backing tracks, the hairdressing and makeup, the choice of presenters and their outfits.

There are even political challenges: who's going to be invited as a VIP guest? Where will he or she sit on the night? Who outranks whom, does nationality count and are there any diplomatic minefields? Who's going to be left out?

And nearer home, which county's scenic waterfall is going to be showcased and which county's ignored?

On her fiftieth birthday, Moya's eighteen-year-old son Mark, who is an artist, gave her a handmade card: 'To the most organised person I know'. 'My nature is to plan. I run my life with lists,' she says. 'I'd had all that great RTÉ training: training to be a broadcasting assistant, training to be a production assistant, training to be a producer/director – they give you fantastic training so you certainly know how to plan!' All this on top of experience as an actress, an additional stint as a TV presenter on a major show in Britain and as the exceptionally efficient secretary to News Features, the peripatetic RTÉ Radio newsroom team who, over the years, have brought us *Morning Ireland, News at One Thirty, World Report* and *This Week*. The woman has some CV.

'I had decided also that I wanted to enjoy it if I could. I knew there would be last-minute crises to deal with – so anything I could get squared away in advance, I should.'

The interval act was one item that was could be organised in advance, and soon after she was given the job, and had sat down to draw up her lists, she began to think about it. She remembered that a couple of years previously, she had been impressed by two dancers, Michael Flatley and Jean Butler, when they had performed separately during a show put on at the National Concert Hall in connection with the celebrations of 'Mayo 5000'. 'John, who was producing that

A lifetime in music: Bill Whelan at the Meteor Music Awards, 2006.

show, had booked them because both had Mayo connections.' Here was a thought: how about putting them on together?

As for the music, she had been discussing with John the concept of using Irish dance in an innovative and exciting way and was mulling over who should compose the music for it, 'and John said, "Look, you can't pass Bill's door."'

She knew Bill Whelan well. 'Bill and John were tremendous friends. Bill had worked on a number of music shows John had worked on – he even had Eurovision experience, having composed Time Dance for a previous interval act.' She asked him to meet her for a cup of coffee.

So, with Whelan, Flatley, Butler, Anúna and the cream of Irish dancers engaged and planning, 'I knew that the Riverdance element of the show was squared away.'

She does not want us to forget the rest of the show that night. 'Because *Riverdance* sort of exploded, all the other elements have been overlooked ever since.' She wants us to remembers the 'fantastic' set designed by Paula Farrell: 'I wanted it urban and neon; in my head, the shape of the Point Theatre informed it.' Paula delivered.

And a great deal of thought went into the opening sequence: 'We used the river as the theme.' She had originally wanted a real, onstage waterway, but this proved too problematic, so she compromised with a thematic depiction of the river flowing outside the theatre's door. She employed Macnas, the iconic Galway street-theatre group, to create the big heads of U2, Joyce et al. 'They were designed specifically for that opening sequence, and they've been used everywhere since. We had the best of everything.'

It did seem that money was no object.

Well, she did exceed the budget set aside for that opening sequence. 'I had to go and get extra money for it and I did that by approaching the then Minister for Finance.' Cleverly, she asked for the help of Harry Crosbie, the Point's proprietor and Bertie's fellow Dub, in making these representations. Bertie coughed up.

Although she was very happy with what she had seen of *Riverdance* in rehearsal, she missed her star turn on the night itself. During the interval, 'I was in a small room at the back calling in the votes of Bosnia Herzegovina – and it kind of took my eye off the *Riverdance* enjoyment moment!'

You see, it was very, very important to get that voting system running smoothly because here, too, she had innovated – and been stubborn – and her neck was on the line. 'I'd had a big head-on battle with the EBU to get away from telephone voting.'

The European Broadcasting Union is the co-operative umbrella organisation to which all the public broadcasters in Europe – and some other countries, such as Israel – belong. They share radio and TV technology, exchange programmes, and run various international competitions. Ireland, in the person of Doherty, wanted, for the first time, to get away from telephone voting and instead use in-vision satellite technology. Her bosses reacted 'delightedly' to the proposal. Technologically, they wanted to be the best. They were thrilled to be the ones pioneering it.'

And so, tail up, she brought her proposal to the EBU – and hit a stone wall. 'Specifically an EBU gentleman.'

From the gentleman's point of view, here was an unheard-of suggestion from a colleen with a gorgeous smile who had somehow been allowed to entertain preposterous and uppity notions. 'He just dismissed me with a flick of his hand. He said "It's going to be too expensive." He said, "Germany, France, the big countries are not going to pay for it." He said, "Forget it!"'

For the next while, assuming that this initial reaction was just a negotiating ploy, she busied herself with other tasks and waited for a formal response. 'I was sure that this man was going to negotiate, that this was progress.'

She was wrong. 'He had just pawned me off. And I thought, You're not going to do that!' The gentleman concerned had no idea that, far from dealing with a colleen, he had locked horns with Donegal Woman.

She and a colleague, Marie Travers, faxed the head of every individual television-station-cum-jury. 'And I will never forget being in the office over a couple of days and the faxes coming back.'

'Yes, we will.'

'Yes, we will.'

'Of course we will.'

'We'd love to.'

'We absolutely will.'

Twenty-nine yesses.

'I'd bypassed him.'

Now, of course, she was daunted. 'You know when you want something and plan it and it looks like it's going to happen? Then you start to worry. Suppose the show is a disaster, the voting is a disaster. Never mind the interval act – that's what you'll be remembered for: "That was the year of the disastrous voting!"'

In the meantime, having left *Riverdance* to its own devices, at which stage did she know exactly what she had on her hands?

'I don't think anyone could have predicted what it turned into,' but during the rehearsal period, there were indications. 'I picked up people's reactions.'

For instance, those of the camera crews. They've seen it all. 'They were all stopping and going –' She whistles. The fizz had begun.

How does she feel now about Flatley, given their highly publicised falling out?

Her reaction is calm and sensible: 'I bumped into him in the Four Seasons in New York a while ago, and we had a very pleasant drink. He is hugely talented – look, *Riverdance* worked for everybody. There was a moment and we all seized it. Remember, Michael wasn't a spring chicken when he was cast; he'd been dancing for thirty years, and he hadn't broken through in the way he deserved.'

Occasionally, still, some columnist with a few inches to fill will bring up the so-called 'feud' between the dancer and the show's creators and will represent the latter as maintaining a grudge. 'The reality is, of course, that one would rather not have any . . .' She searches for a word and fails to find the right one. Then: 'It became very clear after the first year that the show Bill, John and I wanted to sustain wasn't the show Michael wanted to do. That's very clear when you look at what he does. His is a very different type of show. He's done inordinately well with it and it's exactly what he should be doing – but it isn't what we wanted to do. Those creative differences were the key. But there's room for everything.' And because of its unprecedented worldwide success, *Riverdance* became an international calling card for all involved in it, Michael Flatley included.

One of those cards proved not to bring so much luck for the McColgans. They presented it in New York – where they had been very successful with *Riverdance* at Radio City Music Hall – to introduce their enormously ambitious foray into the Broadway shark

Opposite:
Dancing up a storm.

pool with their musical *The Pirate Queen*.

They went across the Atlantic with high hopes and confidence, having contracted writers Alain Boublil and Claude-Michel Schönberg to write the show's book, based on the pair's reputation for *Les Misérables*, *Miss Saigon* – and the less universally popular but critically admired *Martin Guerre*. They had auditioned for and hired what remains, in Moya's opinion, 'the best cast on Broadway'. They invested millions of their own money – and lost the gamble. The critics savaged the show and they closed it prematurely, having played from just 5 April to 17 June 2007.

They had little warning of what was to come. The previews attracted 'stuffed audiences, fantastic response, standing ovations, unbelievable reaction'. As a result, the show's collective panning by the critics came as a severe shock. 'Once the reviews came out it changed everything. What amazed me is that they found nothing good to say.'

Quite a lot of the critics' ire was aimed at the show's writers, who, she says staunchly, are 'wonderful guys, interesting people, very bright, mature men. Claude-Michel's reaction was to tell us this very old Chinese proverb: you fall seven times you get up eight. But they were gutted. I felt quite heartbroken for them and for the cast, who were stunned. They came to us and said, "We're so sorry you were treated like this in our city."

'And when we told them we were closing, we got an ovation from them on stage.'

That premature closing was a 'very tough decision. But the right decision and the only one we could take at the time. It's a tough business, the business of Broadway musicals, and so many of them have failed. We just didn't expect this to be one of them.' It was a hard lesson. 'But life is tough and not everything works.'

As for the home reaction in some quarters to such a public failure by such a successful couple, it could be characterised as gleeful *Schadenfreude* of a particularly Irish hue – à la Charlie McCreevy's thesis. To illustrate: have you heard the one about the two lobster tanks in the French restaurant? Where one of the tanks had a cover over the top and the other did not? A curious punter goes up to the maître d' and asks why this should be. 'Oh,' says the worthy,

'Let me show you how it's done.' Riverdance returns to the Gaiety Theatre, 2005.

shrugging as is his Gallic wont, 'in one tank we 'ave ze French lobsters and in ze ozzer we 'ave ze Irish lobsters. You see, M'sieur, we must keep ze French lobsters covaired, but in ze Irish tank, we do not need a covair, *non*? Because if one lobster tries to climb up, all ze ozzers pull him back down.'

The McColgans, shattered though they were, remain undaunted. '*The Pirate Queen* was an extraordinary journey and I'm incredibly proud of it as a piece of work.' They also remain loyal to Boublil and Schönberg, the setback having served only to deepen the relationship as they all remain on board their project. The Japanese have bought the rights: *The Pirate Queen* will open in Osaka at the end of 2009 and in Tokyo in 2010.

That Broadway disaster, in concert with other factors, had unexpected personal consequences and became part of an internal storm for Moya Doherty. 'The early demise of *The Pirate Queen*, the passing of both my parents, the growing up of my two eldest sons all happened in one big swirl. It seemed that with the gap left in my life by *The Pirate Queen*, I had been given time to look around and see that a lot of other things were no longer there. I was given that time, time that we don't give ourselves any more, to reflect. I'd been working flat out for thirty years and I probably needed to be forced to stop. I find now I don't have any desire to keep going at that pace and so, with a little bit of hindsight, it [the show's American collapse] may not have been the worst thing to happen to me on a personal basis.'

She finds herself now 'at a crossroads. My sister says, "Stay at the crossroads! Don't be running up any road in a hurry."'

One of the factors that will enable this pause in the headlong gallop of her professional life so far is the opportunity to enjoy it without fear. The McColgans have many mansions, and wealth brings choice. They have earned every penny, and Moya remains grounded. 'Money was never a goal. I meet young people nowadays and you ask them,

"What do you want to do?" and they answer, "I want to be famous. I want to be a millionaire by the age of twenty-eight."

'Yes, but what do you want to do?'

They were not always wealthy and have not lost sight of the fact, perhaps courtesy of *The Pirate Queen*, that riches are evanescent. 'The first time I got a taste of money was when we lived in London in the eighties. Remember Ireland in the eighties? It was miserable, divorce referendums and so on. Thank God we were in London for five wonderful years, even if it was Thatcher and the miners' strike. We were cocooned in the television business in London. We were incredibly well paid and the tax was twenty-four per cent. I had money for the first time ever. I saved four thousand pounds in cash! And I bought my car outright for cash!' It's still a wonder to her. 'You'd never have seen the colour of that in Ireland. I bought my little Renault Five and I got a sense – My God! We can pay for a holiday. We can pay our mortgage!'

When they decided to come back to Ireland, and let this decision be known, 'a priest friend of ours rang and said, "Are you mad coming back to this country?" But we wanted kids and the option at the time was move out of London and commute. That wasn't what we wanted.'

Like kids in a sweetshop, they have played with their money and used it with great enjoyment: Tyrone House, where Moya and I meet, replete with etched glass and beautiful wood, is filled with art and sculpture, awards and their own mementoes. There are witty touches too, such as the 'yellow brick road' woven into a carpet in a corridor. They have never taken their good fortune for granted and, in middle age now, are soberly grateful for its benefits: 'A degree of confidence, as you face into ageing. It has allowed us to travel, to support people, to educate our children in a way we wouldn't have been able to.'

They also make sure their sons properly understand that large financial resources are not an intrinsic right but arise as a consequence of graft. 'One four-letter word is very important in our house and that's "work".'

Their son, Mark, was sent to board at an arts college near Boston at the age of fifteen, not on a whim or simply because his parents could afford the 'astronomical' fees but because it was the right school for him. 'It was a big decision for us to be separated from him at such a young age. I don't know if it was the right decision for me as a mother or for John as a father because we missed him during those precious growing-up years. I used to be pretty intolerant in the past of people going on about the empty-nest syndrome: I used to think, Oh, get on with it – but now I understand it. It came early for me.'

And apart from ensuring a good formal education for them, the boys' parents are determined that each will appreciate – or at least be continually exposed to – some aspect of culture or arts: 'Our children may not know who David Beckham is, but they will certainly know Elvis and they'll know Pavarotti!'

Although she typifies the cliché that the harder you work, the luckier you become, Moya does know how fortunate she is now to have an opportunity to cut down for reflection. 'For the first time in my adult life I have time. I called out to see someone last week. And I remember the last time, and every time, I called out to see this person I was rushing, I was on the phone, I was checking three thousand emails. This was the first time I went and just sat with this woman and we were in the moment. And there was no outside drag on my head and I'm thinking, This is absolutely beautiful.

'We are different fifty-year-olds from our mothers and grandmothers. There's so much I want to do, and it's wonderful to have the time to work up and develop proposals, but I don't want to take on anything major right now. We have a number of very healthy projects on the go, none overly demanding or stressful. It's really interesting [to watch the reactions] when people ask me, "What are you doing now?" and I say, "I'm doing nothing. And loving it!" We are defined by what we do and breaking away from that definition is challenging, especially if you have "done" all your life.'

Does John feel the same at this stage?

'John has put three working lifetimes into work. When everyone in RTÉ was doing one project, he was doing three. Because that's his nature. For years I was asking him "When are you going to retire, John?" until I realised it was a ridiculous question. Why am I asking this of a man who clearly has no intention of retiring?'

She returns to her own intersection: 'There's a lot of junk around about ageing where women are concerned. I look at women I admire who are ageing in a certain way and I say, "I want to be able to do the lotus position when I'm seventy, on a beach somewhere with my grey hair flowing in the wind."'

In that wind there will be, no doubt, echoes of those *Riverdance* drums. She remains 'really, really proud' of that creation and never gets tired of hearing its music. She is genuinely astonished at what the show has become, 'completely outside all of our management control, plans, desires and so on. Those that are part of it have taken charge of it and made it their own.

'What is wonderful is the journey we have witnessed of all those young Irish dancers and musicians, singers male and female. They've gone through *Riverdance*, they've met their partners, they've married, they've had babies, they've seen the world. It has dramatically changed my life, John's life, Bill's life, Michael Flatley's life. It has changed the lives of all those who have been with it.'

She also marvels at the opportunity that Fate – and talent and a reputation for organisational skills and hard work – awarded her: 'The timing and the way it happened. Remember, this came out of a public-broadcasting television show. It was never intended to be a

*Winners Paul
Harrington and
Charlie McGettigan.*

theatrical event.'

It morphed because, on being asked to film it as part of a TV special for the following Christmas, she responded, 'I don't want to do it just as a TV show. I think it should be a theatrical show and we'll film that for Christmas.'

And, ever since, *Riverdance* has continued to orbit the world, changing its riders' lives with each pass. It has been very beneficial for a lot of people. It's not life as we know it, Scottie. It hums differently.

And, by the way, the winners of the thirty-ninth Eurovision Song Contest were Paul Harrington and Charlie McGettigan, with the Brendan Graham song, 'Rock 'n' Roll Kids'.

They might have been singing about the McColgans.

Dancing with My Father

Johnny Logan – Champion of Europe!

Yeah, *Riverdance*. Essentially a by-product, albeit a very valuable one, but one that overshadowed that year's song in the public memory. So, let's talk to someone whose three songs have actually won the Eurovision Song Contest – and who has come second with a fourth. Maybe we'll find out what it feels like to have become a Eurovision icon, someone who has, nevertheless, suffered over the years from the kind of smart-alec cynicism that so irritates Charlie McCreevy.

Take this. While riding high in various charts (except in Ireland) with a duet he had recorded with the Ghanaian rap singer, Kaye Styles, he was approached by a tabloid journalist for an interview and gave her a quote or two.

The hack started the resulting piece with: 'Johnny Logan's back! Do you care? No, neither do I . . .'

'She wrote that I'd "jumped into a studio with Kaye Styles as soon as he got back from the Eurovision".' There followed more in that vein, heavy with the implication that Ireland's Johnny was clawing his way back up the pop ladder on Kaye Styles's talented shoulders. 'He never got to the Eurovision, he was only in the National Song Contest. And it was he approached me – not the other way round. And she had the nerve afterwards to ask me for a "follow-up" interview.'

It still smarts. You never get used to it and he doesn't, no matter how many European charts he tops, no matter how many crowned heads – including the Pope's – he has performed for, no matter how many duets or charity songs he has been asked to do with pop (Paul McCartney), rock (Elvis Presley's band, the Jordanaires), or classical (Montserrat Caballé) royalty.

Well, he is back home in Ireland, snatching a four-day break from shows all over Europe and promoting his albums: 'I'm number one in every country in Scandinavia and I've just gone double platinum.' This is in addition to whizzing forwards and back across the Atlantic to facilitate the construction phase of new recordings, laying down tracks in different venues, based on which studio does what kind of music best.

Opposite:
'What's another year?'
19 April 1980.

There are a lot of people in Scandinavia. There are a lot of people in Holland and even more in Germany. They buy a lot of music. Why should he care what they think of him in Ireland?

His home is here, in Ashbourne, County Meath. It's where his wife and three sons live. And, as with many other artists, whether they admit it or not, the home crowd's opinion matters most.

We do remember, don't we, that first Eurovision win in 1980 with Shay Healy's song, 'What's Another Year?'? And the second with his own 'Hold Me Now' in 1987? And the third, with Linda Martin singing his 'Why Me?' in 1992? (Not to mention Linda's second place

Winning with 'Why Me?' – Linda Martin, 1992.

with his 'Terminal Three'.)

That first win led him to where he is now. Having survived a less than sure-footed initial post-Eurovision career, he is now one of the few winners, relatively speaking, whose hopes of an international career have come to fruition. Abba. Buck's Fizz, who in Dublin won for the UK in 1981. Nicole, Germany's winner a year later, continues to be a major star on the European continent. Bobby Socks (for Norway in 1985) are still around, so is Sandra Kim, and, of course, Johnny's win in 1987 brought someone called Céline Dion to Dublin a year later to take the prize for Switzerland. I have a soft spot for Lordi – but Riva, anyone? Toto Cotugno?

Johnny Logan wasn't the first Irish winner, of course. Dana Rosemary Scallon did it for us with 'All Kinds Of Everything' and we were delighted, thrilled even, but she was still a teenager. *Cailín gleoite.* We like shy people. Sonya was the same. No matter how many races or how much money she won, she was just that lovely girl from Cobh with the bashful smile – she'd remind you of Lady Di.

In general, with some notable National Treasures like Maeve Binchy – no palaces in Monaco, just a grand little cottage out there in Dalkey – we're not mad about celebrating success if it involves wealth (hey – it's Charlie McCreevy again). And we don't like people who push themselves, even if they have to do so to stay afloat in a competitive market. Johnny Logan understands this very well. There is no doubt that he is doing well, but frequently, when talking about himself or his successes, he will preface what he says with 'Now I don't want this to sound egotistical . . .'

It is a sunny day and Seán Patrick Michael Sherrard is sitting at my kitchen table. Dogs like him. Instead of running up the stairs as usual to hide from strangers, our shy collie bitch is sitting at his feet. Our old collie dog is there too, splayed because of his arthritis, but doing his best to make his eyes twinkle in the hopes of catching a biscuit crumb from this rich man's table.

His looks have held up. Viewing again the video of that first win, his face was that of a first-communicant (to match the immaculate white suit) but now the presentation, albeit off-duty, is slightly rumpled, the expression that of a man who has lived.

Born in Australia, the cliché 'larger than life' can be applied to his personality and physical presence: he is a tall fellow with a big frame, but that's not why everything around him seems to shrink. At fifty-three he exudes, these days, the kind of easy confidence that comes with having fought through and survived many disappointments, his own and others' naïveté, mismanagement, starry triumphs, weeks, months and years of derision and scoffing, a lot of flattery, excessive celebrationss and a strand of deep sorrow.

The confidence is not overweening – he checks it with self-deprecation, but it is knowing: for example, he took a long time to accept the invitation to do that McDonald's commercial, the one where, in a (slightly larger) white suit, he bursts in on 'the girls' with a self-parodying – but pitch perfect – version of 'Hold Me Now'. He finally agreed to sign up only when it became clear from the script 'that I would be part of the joke, not the joke. It's not slagging. When I'm coming home through Passport Control or Customs, I'm asked by the guy for a Big Mac. It's great.' And, yes, he does have 'perfect

The thumbs-down option pic, just in case! Johnny with Shay.

pitch', that rarity granted to very few, whereby a singer or musician without being played a particular note on a piano or other instrument can hit it exactly.

He has developed a stock reaction to the 'Are you still singin', Johnny?' remarks thrown at him, usually as he passes in and out of Dublin airport: 'Yeah, I tried the ballet dancin' and it didn't work!'

What didn't work was his early apprenticeship as an electrician. He wanted nothing less than a professional singing career, just like his dad's. Charles Sherrard, professional name Patrick O'Hagan, was a lyric Irish tenor with a popular repertoire and international reputation. His career included three appearances at the White House in Washington.

So, while he was ostensibly learning how to distinguish differently coloured wires, Patrick O'Hagan's son auditioned for, and won, leads in several successful musicals here (*Adam and Eve*, *Joseph and the Amazing Technicolour Dreamcoat*) and he was launched.

He had tried many times for the Eurovision Song Contest, always writing, rarely singing. But then Shay Healy asked him to sing 'What's Another Year?' – and was responsible for a day when we could cheer Ireland to the rafters. 'You probably remember it better than me' – he's referring to the prolonged bout of celebration that followed his win in The Hague.

I don't, actually. I wasn't there. But I do know full well how those celebrations go. I was in Brussels for the second win with 'Hold Me Now'. I called the *Tribune* news desk immediately after his performance to alert the paper that it had blown the audience away. 'Are we in danger of winning this thing?' asked the guy on duty that Saturday night, and even over a noisy phone line, I could hear his incredulity.

On the night of the 1980 win, Logan remembers, 'very strongly and vividly', the immediate aftermath of the competition: 'being led round and doing interviews and so on . . .'

What did it feel like?

'It's very hard to describe what it felt like. In those days the reaction was huge. Unbelievable. The record companies were all trying to get you to go immediately to their different territories to do TV shows and so on, but I had to turn them down because I was aware I had to go back to Ireland first. I had all my managers, and all these people, in tow. Trying to give me advice. But they didn't know what they were doing any more than I did.

'It wasn't a blur, exactly – for instance, I can remember sitting on a barrel at the back of a bar in The Hague talking to a journalist. I can remember Louis [Walsh] and me going out much later.' They went to a club and were approached by two ladies and, as far as he remembers, 'The best thing I can say about them is that their tattoos were spelt correctly! One had a very deep voice and used the men's loo . . .

'It was all very funny. The way Shay used to dress at the time . . . And I couldn't sleep that night with all the adrenalin and excitement. The next morning I was in the swimming-pool and my brother, Mick, walked straight into it, completely dressed, with a pint of beer in his hand.'

In that pool, the brothers proceeded to have a prophetic conversation: 'The shit's going to hit the fan now. Something's going to happen. There are too many people involved.'

What he remembers of coming back on the plane is not all the champagne, 'I didn't drink very much in those days', but the communal pride. 'They were all so proud, Noel Kelehan and Shay and Dymphna and Pat Rice and Anne Piaf Bush . . .' Dymphna was Shay Healy's wife; Pat Rice and Anne Bushnell were two of the backing singers. ('The Bush', as the latter is affectionately known in the business, is still going strong with her solo career based around the songs of Edith Piaf.)

'When I got off the plane, there were thousands of people in the airport. I walked out and my uncle Gregory and my aunt Lucy were at the bottom of the steps, waiting for me – and all the posters, "We love Johnny", and so on . . .' But he cringes every time archive footage of that airport arrival is shown: 'That hair! And the shiny black leather tie, the real thin one, and the white leather shirt and black leather waistcoat . . .'

After a great to-do on the tarmac, 'I didn't make the press conference. They took me through the wrong door.'

This lapse occurred apparently for security reasons, not least because of Logan's puppyish reaction to the crowds. 'I was hugely excited, an unnatural buzz. I wanted to go out to them. I wanted to share. I wanted to go up to the people and show them how I felt. Hug everybody. Obviously this bothered the security guy.'

So the wrong door was opened and he found himself locked

outside with just two or three of 'his own' people around him, 'and people pulling me from right and left . . . I wasn't afraid because it wasn't me. It was like I was behind a camera and looking at me through the lens. I can really remember that. They were touching me but they weren't touching me because I was somewhere at the back of me. Everything was slow.

'Eventually I got to a car and they put me in the back and we drove off to Ashbourne. And there was a civic reception . . .'

He speaks with the observational recall of a writer: he's seeing it all now, counting slowly, 'My father-in-law and my wife were sitting there, and my mother-in-law – they'd made a stage on the back of a

'If the singing doesn't work out, there's always the dancing.' Homecoming, Dublin Airport, first Eurovision win.

big lorry. And I was sat up there and they made speeches. And they gave me an award from the town. Adam, who's now twenty-eight, was one year old and he was sitting on my knee. I got up and gave a speech. And we had dinner in the Ashbourne House. And next day I was doing TV. I did *Top of the Pops* in London, I was number one, it was my birthday . . .'

He snaps back: 'That was Part One. They did the same thing in 1987 and 1992 – they brought Linda [Martin] along for that one!'

By his own account, after the excitement and flattery and TV gigs abated and the world turned to matters other than the 1980 Eurovision Song Contest, both Johnny Logan and Seán Patrick Michael Sherrard were floundering. 'After 1980, I didn't bring it off. You can put this down to mismanagement – which is what it was, basically. There was no follow-on. Six months after the Eurovision I was still doing television shows with "What's Another Year?". I should have been in a recording studio two days afterwards, putting together an album.' But by the time he had released the follow-up, with the hostage-to-sarcasm title of 'Save Me' it was too late. To add to the misery, 'We couldn't get *Top of the Pops* because all the musicians were on strike.'

Logan, who has a quirky funny bone, sees the humorous side of this. To promote the song – and, remember, he was still the reigning Eurovision winner – he was asked to appear on the daytime TV show *Pebble Mill*. The set was positioned in front of a large picture window, a real one with acres of glass. 'And I was sitting in there being interviewed and all the musicians were walking up and down outside the window. It was like a Monty Python sketch. I can laugh at it now but I had four and a half horrible years.'

His problem was that there were too many people in charge, each and all with differing so-called 'strategies' for capitalising on his win but no one having much of a clue about how to put flesh on any idea.

Least of all himself. He does take some of the blame for the mess: 'I never put my hand up and said, "Something's wrong" until those six months had passed.'

He doesn't want to go into it, these days. In a relatively recent interview with Gerry Ryan, 'Gerry was trying to get me to have a go at [his managers and agents] the Hands, Tommy Hayden and so on. To say bad things about the past. But all that's got to be let go now. If you look back at that time, and I can do it now with a clearer head, they've got families who don't need to be dragged into all this now. Nobody deliberately set out to get me or to ruin me, so just let it go . . .'

Throughout, he never stopped writing songs, at home, in hotel rooms, anywhere he found himself. One, 'Hold Me Now' worked 'like a dream. And everything changed for the better.'

The instant and major recollection is not connected to the Saturday night in Brussels, but to the National Song Contest in Ireland some weeks beforehand: 'Walking off that stage after singing it and seeing Ailis [his wife] crying in the wings.'

Ailis's tears had been prompted by a release of tension and stress. 'She'd seen the seven years that I'd been through and she'd been through them with me. And I put my arm around her and said, "It's OK now, it's all right now, everything's going to be all right now." And it has been.

Consequently, the Johnny Logan who went to Brussels in 1987 was a very different man from the dazzled kid who'd gone to The Hague in 1980. For a start, he had Louis Walsh looking after him and Louis knew what he was doing. He's still in touch with Louis: 'We text each other a lot. He mixes in a different circle, England and Ireland. I'm more Scandinavia, Germany, Belgium, Holland . . .' He laughs fondly. 'He's the type, if he was due to read the nine o'clock news, he'd come on at five to nine: "I couldn't wait to tell ya . . ."'

Seán Sherrard is headstrong, and to ask for advice has always been

On the way to Eurovision, 1987.

a difficult thing for him to do. In the case of 'Hold Me Now', however, he overcame this trait to consult Shay Healy and Bill Whelan about what to do with the song. 'And the biggest decision I made was to sing it myself. It wasn't ego. I didn't "hear" anyone singing it better than me. I knew everything about that song, I knew where it came from. I'd edited it down from six minutes to three specifically for the Eurovision.'

And when he won, he was ready. 'I turned my contracts over from Sony England to Sony Germany.'

The world of charts had changed, however, and while the second winning song outsold the first two to one, six million to three million, getting to number one in the UK, which had been automatic for Eurovision winners in the past and which seems to be the 'real' goal in the minds of Irish acts, was not to be. 'Whitney Houston kept me off for three weeks with "I Wanna Dance With Somebody".'

Still, it didn't kill him this time. Nor did he implode when he fell out of those UK charts much sooner than he had in 1980. 'Johnny Logan, the Tour of Europe' was by then well under way, and reality for him since has been concerts and albums going platinum and gold all over Europe; it is also working the 'gala' circuit, on which organisations contract big-name artists to entertain staff and guests at conferences and other such events. His particular circuit includes people like Gloria Gaynor, Tom Jones and Jennifer Rush. 'Companies had fortunes back in the eighties to spend on the artists for these galas. It's not the same now' – but it does remain lucrative enough to provide Logan with a good living, and an opportunity, even here, to do some creative work. 'I became very good at this. Belgium, Holland – I have different programmes for each area. I work with big bands with brass sections. I do all the scores and there's never any repetition.'

All the musicians in his own band, his core group, are from Jutland, while in Germany he is working with a group called the Voices Project – Paul Young, Tony Hadley (former lead singer of Spandau Ballet) and himself: 'That's interesting. Each one of us does a set and then we all sing together. This, too, involves a big band with a brass section.'

It's time for the Muppet question. So what does it feel like, Johnny, really deep inside, when you're singing? Especially when you're on track, knowing that everything is congruent: instinct, voice, music, words?

He's polite enough not to wince. 'Oh, that's easy. You don't always do it right, but when you do, you feel this huge emotion inside you. It's whatever you're singing about. It's the depth of what you're singing about. It can be about a story. For me it's like that guy [Harry Chapin] who sings that song ['Colours'] about the reds and greens of flowers, and so on. It's songs that have meaning. They can be as corny as shite, but just at that moment when you're singing them, they're perfect. You've made a connection inside of yourself. Grace. I hope I'm not going to sound pretentious, but it's like God is with you. You can feel a great sense of love. You know you're on the button. God smiles at you.'

He fears he has committed the ego sin, or at least the pretension one. 'I've had so many ups, and downs as well, songs that didn't work. I recorded some great songs, but to be honest, I recorded shite as well. Looking back, I made lots of records I shouldn't have made. I did them on the advice of others so that I could look after my family. But one thing I have learned. Fame comes and goes. I've been famous, I've been unfamous, I've been famous again. I loved what I did before I became famous. I still love it now. I love it more now that I'm involved in production. The music is the constant.'

He speaks ardently about the arranging and production side of bringing out albums: 'My passion for eighties music has returned. For a long time I was looking for a second "Hold Me Now", and I have it. It's called "When A Woman Loves A Man", so I know I can do that. But I did this album of Irish music that I grew up with and suddenly it's platinum in all these countries, and gold, and I'm thinking, The world has gone full circle for me, I'm back where I started as a musician.'

It was as a musician that at three o'clock one morning during 1992 he rang Linda Martin's house. 'I've got the song down to three minutes,' he yelled, when the phone was picked up. 'Linda, I think you can win the Eurovision with this' – but it wasn't Linda who had answered. It was her partner, who flatly refused to wake her up. 'Very frustrating. Other people don't work the same hours. I did my best work at night. On my own. With a good bottle of wine.'

'Why Me?' won for Ireland in Malmö, Sweden. That night he flew there from Germany where he had been promoting a new album: how was it to watch, rather than be out there under the lights, the focus of millions of people?

'It was much easier to sit in the background. There was still excitement. I was half cut, anyway. We were backstage by the champagne fountain, and every time we got twelve points, there was another shot of champagne thrown down.'

At the time of this interview, it has been 'two years and four months' since he had drunk his last drink. Such exactitude is usually, although in fairness not always, a pointer. Did he stop drinking because he thought he had a problem?

'It depends on the definition of "problem". I always managed to do my job.'

The definitions of alcoholism are myriad. One is that if alcohol is causing problems in any part of your life, personal, professional or social, you should start worrying about it.

'In my case it wasn't causing problems. But I wasn't dealing with the problems in my life, and that had been going on for a long time. I don't want this to sound egotistical but I was making records and trying to do my pop-star stuff and trying to do my song-writing and all the rest of it – and I found that I could do all of that and drink. That was the worst aspect.

'You'd have a drink at the airport, a drink on the plane, a drink when you'd land – a drink before the show, drink during the show, drink after the show – and first thing in the morning you'd start all over again. I found myself having no limits. I was never very good at boundaries or limits anyway, that was never one of my strong points. But drink never affected my work and I was able to work my way through it.'

The jargon would have it that this is the classic behaviour of a 'functioning' alcoholic, and coming up to Christmas 2006, he made the decision. 'I said to my family and people close to me, "I'm going to stop drinking on the third of January."'

In preparation for the big step, he had significantly cut his alcohol intake while working in Cologne. He had it all planned. 'I'll be going home the following day. I'll have just a few drinks at the airport. Christmas then, and on New Year's Day I'll have just a few drinks before I slow down on the second – for the third.'

He stopped on schedule.

Is he sure he doesn't mind all of this being known in public?

On the contrary: 'I'm very proud of the fact that I was able to stop drinking. And the way I stopped. No detox or anything else.' He did go to a counsellor for a while. 'I thought I'd find the reason why I was drinking and the guy explained to me, "You may never find the reason."'

There aren't that many deliriously happy artists about – isn't internal turmoil and dissatisfaction an integral part of what keeps creative people in every discipline, song-writing included, striving to create?

'Maybe. Very possibly. I've never been satisfied. But how would I know what peace of mind is when I've never had peace of mind?'

So, in the absence of alcohol, he has made do with ice cream 'and retail therapy. I've got to love shopping!' And, yes, he misses it. Sometimes more than others. 'I was in Cape Town, the sun was beating down. It was still the first year, and myself and my manager went to a restaurant in the harbour and we were having a lovely fish meal.

'And the waiter came up: [in a perfect Afrikaner accent] "Would you loike a gloss of woine with thet?"

'"No, thanks."

'"You're a Muslim?"

'"No. I'm Irish."

'"You're an Irish Muslim!"'

He cracks up.

But this interview now gets difficult – for the interviewer. He has no objections at all to talking openly about alcohol, or about his deep and abiding love for his late dad – he's only too eager, actually.

We have been talking for almost two hours with the sunshine flickering in the trees outside, and the collies, continuing to glance half-heartedly at the biscuits on the table, ambling in and out of the open door. He is very relaxed. But when we move to the subject of Patrick O'Hagan, it becomes so evident that the son's love of the father and the depth of loss he experienced at the father's death in 1993 are still so deeply felt that to pick at them would be trespassing across the boundaries he has such difficulty in setting.

Except to show you this. Seán Sherrard's dad suffered from a debilitating joint affliction that made it difficult for him to manage his own stage wear. He toured extensively during his career and so his son, when he was old enough, toured with him as assistant and dresser. The relationship between a performer and any trusted assistant is close, and that between performer and dresser particularly so. When they had time on their hands between shows, they sang together in dressing rooms . . .

And there is one more image I will use. Patrick O'Hagan had moved to Australia in the hope that his health would benefit from its drier climate. As an adult, his son visited as often as he could.

He made one such visit during a period when, between the 1980 and 1987 wins, he was flailing and desperate, rudderless in life and work. Trailed by a TV documentary team making a programme about him, he emerged from the aircraft and, seeing his father there, waiting for him, Johnny Logan, uncaring about TV cameras or who in the world saw, put his head on Patrick O'Hagan's shoulder and, in his father's arms, wept like a child. 'It's all there. The camera was circling us.'

We'll leave it to them. But we'll let you 'hear' the song that feeds off that image. I hope you can imagine how, a cappella and in almost throwaway fashion, he sang it for the collies and me on a spring afternoon in County Meath:

I go dancing with my father through the streets of yesterday
To the music of tomorrow and the words I heard him say
Through the halls of laughter to the love behind his smile
Then I danced with him a moment and I listened for a while
And did I tell you that I miss you more each day?
How you never really went away?
I go dancing with my father
Through the streets of yesterday
To the songs that as a man I've learned to play

I give him a lift to the village, where Ailis is to pick him up and drive him back to Ashbourne. When I get home again, the house seems very quiet, even though the radio is on and the phone is ringing.

Had Johnny Logan really been in my house?

Then I see the Logan-sized gap at the table. Somehow, after all his 'ups and downs', as he calls them, this endlessly enthusiastic, sweet-natured, flawed, self-critical, open-hearted and incautious man retains the God-given ability to inhabit his space, effortlessly attaining the art of what my old nemesis in theatre, the director Frank Dermody, used to call 'displacing air'. This has something to do with the innate presence and vitality of a star performer and, like perfect pitch, is a facility granted to very few. It can be enhanced by experience but never induced.

Jack and Jessie are wondering when he's coming back. Even if he never ever gives them a biscuit.

Johnny Logan's interview had run for longer than I had anticipated so I was late for a formal dinner that evening. As the main course was being served, a man from the penguin-suited row on the opposite side of the table asked politely what particular project had detained me. Equally politely, those beside him listened while I explained the premise for this book, days we all remember, Logan's emergence, blinking, into the harsh daylight of Dublin airport, the Pope's visit, Ray Houghton's ball into the English net and so on . . .

They sat up. 'Sport? Well, I hope you're going to do The Shot,' said one, while the others nodded in sage recognition.

The wha'?

'The Shot! Did you never hear of The Shot?'

They galvanised, interrupting each other in their eagerness to recount in detail the story of one of the most heroic moments in the history of golf. One even offered kindly to procure a video of that triumph for me so I could see it for myself. (He subsequently went to a lot of trouble and effort to find a copy – ultimately without success.)

This shot was taken, apparently, at an English golf course called the Belfry in 1989 when, during the intercontinental contest for the Ryder Cup, it was pivotal in securing victory for Europe against the USA. Having converted me to the amazingness of this, they then forgot all about me, books et al, and for the next twenty minutes were immersed in discussions about where their hero had gripped. How he had gripped. How he had measured. Where his eyes had been, where his shoulders had been relative to his feet. How he had stood. How he had swung and probably how he had breathed – but by that stage, I had been so far forgotten that I had turned away to talk to one of my nearer neighbours.

I knew, though, that I had to meet this guy.

So this one's about golf, folks. It's about more, too. It's about courage and determination and survival. About old-fashioned family values, love and loyalty.

Little Candles in Bean Tins
Christy Junior Comes of Age

'His swing is a gift from God and he can hit the ball a country mile . . .' Those words were uttered about Christy O'Connor Senior, known affectionately in golf circles, I am reliably informed, as 'Himself', idol of his nephew, Christy Junior. By most accounts, the accolade could apply also to the nephew, driver of The Shot, but he would not think so. 'I dream of being as good as my uncle but I know I'll never be better.'

Uncle and nephew were turned out from the same mould. In 2007, when an honorary doctorate from University College Galway was being bestowed on Junior, Senior got one too. The younger 'cannot even begin to tell you what that meant to me. First of all, I got the freedom of the city of Galway. I love the city and I love the West of Ireland. To have that was fabulous. And then to be given the doctorate with my uncle . . .' Words fail him.

As for the uncle, his comment about the nephew was that 'It took me eighty-three years to get him to UCG.' There will be a lot about Senior in this piece. 'He's a living god to me.'

Big and bluff with the stride and bloom of the outdoors, Christy O'Connor Junior settles at the low coffee table in the bar of the Ballsbridge, formerly the Berkeley Court Hotel. He is at ease, but around him, the plush room seems a little claustrophobic, the upholstery of his chair inappropriate. He may have travelled the world in sophisticated company and may now be making a terrific living creating golf courses at home and abroad but it feels as though he belongs on a hard chair at a country kitchen *céilidhe*, or standing on the deck of a Galway hooker, white cap firmly secured against a fresh wind.

Previous:
The job is done:
Christy triumphs
over Fred Couples,
Ryder Cup,
The Belfry.

We'll get to The Shot in due course but, first, tea for him.

I get my defence in early – the one concerning not having a clue about golf. He'd probably know that anyhow: he's thorough. I've done my own browsing and I know at least that this man eats, sleeps and drinks his game. It is more than a sport to him. It's heritage, family duty, a vocation worthy of a monk. It's a skill hard-earned from the time he was a small boy, when he spent night after night chipping and putting on the greens conveniently located behind the family home in Knocknacarra, Co. Galway. 'We were born on the edge of the golf course.'

He didn't chip alone. Each evening, when the members and guests cleared off home, having enjoyed their rounds and subsequent haw-hawing in the clubhouse of the Galway Golf Club, the invasion began. Like nocturnal animals, troops of small boys from the village scurried on to the deserted greens to join the O'Connors, who had only to climb over their back wall to be already there. 'The whole village played golf, especially at night. That time there was nothing else. No toys or anything. We'd play up to midnight.' And if the moon was absent or not bright enough, 'We would light little candles and put them in bean tins on the greens.'

The authorities knew what was happening, but turned a blind eye, confident that no damage would be done to their swards. 'We knew the etiquette.'

They knew because, for cash, they caddied. 'That was our spare income and our pocket money and we often had to bring it home, too', fees and tips being in many cases an essential part of a village household budget.

From an early age Christy knew the value of a shilling. 'I built a little shop with my mum. I bought my first car when I was thirteen.'

Eh? Did he drive it?

'I certainly did,' with no hindrance from the law. He thinks now this may have been because he was performing an essential public service with his car – in summer, for instance, using it to carry 'crates and crates' of milk around the huge caravan park nearby. (Or it may have been because this was the West of Ireland, where the laws of the Pale did not apply.) Anyhow, 'It gave us a wonderful income and the two of us ran that little shop until all hours of the night.'

In summers therefore, bean-tin practice was curtailed but during every other season, for the boy Christy and for Eugene, Frank and Seán, three of his seven brothers (he has one sister) it felt 'absolutely natural' to spend every spare minute on those greens, however late the hour. Although Christy was the one destined to join the tour, all four became golf professionals, Eugene at a club in Spain, Frank in Germany and Seán, the eldest, in the Bahamas, teaching there for 30 years before coming home to retire. During those boyhood years, Senior's very public success was no small spur to keep them all in training – and basking vicariously in his glory: 'hearing on the radio how my uncle was doing, hearing he'd won another Irish tournament because he used to win most Irish tournaments. My uncle was a local hero in our village.

'During the off-season, I'd play golf twice a day if I could and if I was let. I had the pro's heart broken: Bob Wallace was our king in Galway. Wonderful man. One day he said to me, "You're going to England tomorrow. Tell your parents."'

Bob Wallace's son Kevin and Christy left the next day for their first golf jobs, Christy's at a club in South Shields for a wage of three pounds a week: 'I couldn't even afford the bus to work.' But this was northern England where miens are stony but hearts buttery, especially in those breasts of those golf-club members who see that their young trainee pros are hungry. 'They were really kind. Bringing us for a meal and so on.'

Having got his foot on the golfing ladder, Junior returned to Ireland after eighteen months, this time to his dream job: assistant professional to his revered relative at Royal Dublin. In this he was replacing his brother, who was moving on to the Bahamas.

Royal Dublin was no sinecure. The uncle made him practise, and run, and practise again, until he started 'playing quite nicely'. Next stop was Holland in 1968 to be junior coach to young players the same age as himself – and then he came back to a job as 'full pro at Carlow Golf Club. That was where I really started to practise my golf. Ten hours a day for seven years.'

Did you know (skip, golfers!) that, in the olden days, club professionals had to make the clubs they sold in the clubhouse shop? 'It was fantastic to watch them. I never made the heads but my uncle did.

'You got a block of wood – just the size of that teapot there. Square. And now you had to turn that into a golf club. It was wonderful to watch them. The four corners off first,' he shapes the block between his hands, demonstrating, 'you rounded it out, pared the back, drilled. And then you stained them – that took more than a week. Stained them higher and higher and higher, and then the polishing would start. Gorgeous piece of workmanship. I have loads of them at home.' He lets the imaginary block fall.

As for the grips, 'Nowadays it's so simple. You just have to push them over the club. You put them in a vice with a bit of tacky paper and just slip them on. In the old days you had to build them up with cloth underneath and then you got the leather grip and wrapped it round and round. Each would take you probably two hours. But it stayed for ever.'

When he was in Bundoran as a pro, Christy O'Connor Senior had to do all of this by day. At night, by moonlight, he practised his golf until two in the morning. The nephew, his brothers and village pals made their own clubs for bean-tin practice from the shafts, heads and grips discarded in the tip maintained by Bob Wallace. 'It was a very clean tip, may I add. We would go there and put them together for ourselves. Yeah, golf is my life. It's everything.'

He stopped playing competitively for complex reasons. He is fifty-nine at the time of this interview and well into his follow-on career as a golf-course designer, but at the time he quit the senior tour, he was still playing well. Had the thrill gone out of it?

'No. Thrill, no. But I wasn't putting in the work. You have to practise. Crazy hours. The longer you've been playing, the harder you have to practise. Langer [Bernhard, German] does eight hours every day. He starts at eight and finishes at five, religiously every day. I wasn't doing that much but I was doing five or six. Then I'd whittled

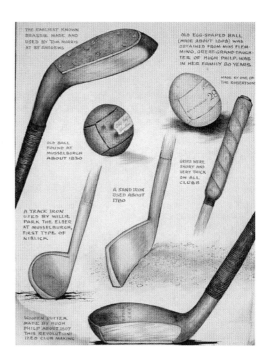

Craftsmanship: Early golf clubs, putters and balls.

it down to an hour. And then it was gone.'

Motivation lost?

'The hunger. I would hate to play tournaments and not to win. I would never go down there if I didn't think I could win. Gee whiz, winning is everything. Coming down to that eighteenth hole, thousands of people standing up and clapping – that's what I call "golf".'

The demotivation did not happen because he no longer had the capacity to win tournaments. In fact, he was enjoying some of the best golf of his life, winning and being placed at senior events on the US tour during 1999, culminating in victory at the Senior British Open in 2000. Cumulatively, he had earned massively more than he had earned in any year previously.

Winning at golf, or at least aiming to die trying, had become the palliative drug of choice for Christy O'Connor Junior, because in 1998 his son, Darren, along with two others, had been killed in a road accident after a 400-mile round trip. He had driven his mother's BMW to see his girlfriend in Killarney. He crashed when he was just a quarter of an hour from home. In the aftermath of the tragedy, his broken-hearted father threw himself into work, 'practising like a demon' and, convinced that Darren was watching over him, playing like an angel.

Ten years on, he finds it 'very, very tough' to talk about the event, and not just because the boy who died was his beloved son. That, of course. But what makes it all the harder for someone who treats golf as the staff of life is his conviction that the boy 'had an incredible future ahead of him' in the sport; continuing in the O'Connor family tradition, Senior had taken him under his wing and had tipped him: 'Yes, you have one.'

Christy Junior had been delighted, naturally, but not surprised. 'He was running, working out. He was much longer than me off the tee, he had a huge, steely temperament. He had just become under-seventeen champion in Ireland, and even at that age, he had got beaten by only one shot in the under-twenty-one championship. We were both ready to go to the States, me on the senior tour, him on a scholarship to start his golfing career. He was going to be the number one of the clan – the number one of the O'Connors.'

It takes 'a little bit of the pain away' to remember that although their son's life was short, Christy and his wife Ann had made it a good one for him. 'We used to go down with the kids to Dingle. I'd light fires and we'd cook full meals. Not just a sandwich. And people'd say to me, "Are you not practising?" I'd practise like hell when I got back – but I think you have to live those days and I'm glad I did, and my kids are glad I did, and I built houses for them – and they say I gave them a good life.'

They also brought their children away with them on the tours 'as much as we could, at least once a year – for instance, to South Africa. And that was the great thing about my late son, he had a safari, he'd been to the Bahamas with my brother, he'd been to Disney World – he saw a lot of stuff.'

The last time Christy and his son were together on a golf course was when the teenager was there with the rest of his family to watch the final putt of one of the two Kenyan Opens that Junior won. 'He ran onto the green. I had all five there that day, my daughter, also Ann, my two sons and my wife and, unfortunately, that was the end of his tournaments because then he was killed. That'll be the biggest hole in my heart for the rest of my life.' This is why, when people ask him if the Ryder Cup event in 1989 was the highlight of his career, he disabuses them. Because of his son's death, 'the Kenya Open means an awful lot to me. It will always be huge in my heart.'

On the day we meet, Darren's father is freshly broken-hearted, having within the previous few days buried his beloved eldest brother Seán, who had died of cancer at the age of sixty-five. 'Such a lovely man. He could not disagree with you: "That's right, you're right, Christy!"'

When the diagnosis was made they both had difficulty coming to terms with it. 'My brother and I went to every church ever made. You'd see the poor guy up on the altar, just begging. It makes you kind of think, when you see what happened to my son and my brother . . .' He is making an attempt to be (relatively) matter-of-fact, but it doesn't work and he retreats to the safety of golf.

Christy wins the 1992 Dunhill British Masters.

'You spend so long practising, you suffer practising, and the sense that you might win is the pay-off: you're getting back at all those long, long hours.' He relives the feeling: 'Wow! Coming to that eighteenth hole!'

And yet, thrilling though it is, that final thrust is 'probably the worst part for your body. Those last nine holes. It's the most nerve-racking part of any tournament. You hate it but you love it. Winning from the last nine holes is very, very hard. Holding on. Trying to hold on. You've played three rounds of nine holes and now you have nine holes left for four rounds. See?'

I don't. But I don't want to wreck his flow with a girly interrogation of what was probably obvious if I'd had the sporting intelligence. With some help later, I think I've subsequently worked it out. (Skip again, golfers! The next two paragraphs!)

Every tournament runs over seventy-two holes. The cut – between the top scorers who will go on to the final and those who won't – is made after the first thirty-six.

You've survived the cut and you've thirty-six holes to play now in earnest. Two eighteen-hole rounds, four sets of nine holes, two out from and two back to the clubhouse. Those last nine, when 'you have nine holes left for four rounds', you're playing the zenith of all seventy-two, pre- and post-cut. Get it?

'Coming down the stretch, it's a very tough time but it's a wonderful time.'

It's more mental than physical?

'Oh, God, yes. Golf is eighty per cent mental and twenty per cent physical.'

He does not miss his competitive playing days. 'People say, "Oh, come on, you've another ten tournaments in you." So what? I've represented Ireland in every single trophy you can play in and, yes, you can go on. But go on for what? To be the oldest player?

'That means nothing.'

To be the oldest player who wins something?

'That means nothing. There are a lot of young players coming along, they need a place on the tour. You take the US Masters, and if you win that you can play for ever. I see guys going out there at seventy years of age, can't hit a cow in the arse with a banjo. And there's some poor young guy next on the list. He should be playing. I gave it everything I could for all those years.'

The circuit gave him a lot back and, in his view, made up for a lack of formal education. 'I couldn't spend valuable time doing formal study but I've always spent a lot of time among people who knew a lot. Especially playing pro-ams, you'd meet people from all walks of life and you'd your ears open. I learned as much as I could about countries. I took notes. I did a bit of photography. I was very diversified – and I enjoyed the social life. You have to live too, you know!'

In his view, bereavement notwithstanding, as a professional golfer, he has had the best of all possible worlds. But now that's over. Next business: design, in which he can live his life by the laws of not just business and competition with big-name rival designers (Whose golf course is the best? Mine is!) but nature.

'Living with nature.' He's delighted with the description. 'Yeah, I love that.'

So who does he admire? (Need I ask?)

'My uncle, who's been the greatest inspiration to us all. Ten Ryder Cups without missing a year. That's where we all came from, one after the other, from a small farm. He took us all into the game.'

OK – the uncle is a given. But other than the uncle?

'I suppose, internationally, Jack Nicklaus was my great guy. He was such a wonderful golfer. He still holds the record – Tiger has a long way to go yet before he beats it. Wonderful power of work and concentration, wonderful mind, huge heart. Great stomach for the game.

have to stay over for the next two days doing nothing. And th
place you want to be is on a golf course where you've just faile
don't want to be there. You want to be miles from there – un
next year when you're back again.'

It has happened to him 'lots of times. But I think two cuts in
is the worst I've had. You can get a bad run, though. I've seer
going seven cuts in a row, eight cuts in a row, and that'
destroying. I've seen it break up families. Because the paren
believing in their sons I've seen double mortgages on homes j
keep the sons going – and we could have told them that their so
going nowhere but we daren't. It's terrible.'

Wouldn't everyone be better off if you did dare? After all,
young Walter Mittys are courageous, yes, but they're gamblii
their lives, and on their parents' lives if they're being staked
out such a precarious profession.

'It's tough to tell someone that you don't see him going dow
road. Because it's not your business. You could tell the pai
maybe, if you're asked. I've been asked and I've got myself in tro
I was asked once by a very good friend. And I knew it had al
involved thousands and thousands of pounds in expenses but
couldn't see the young man going on. That man asked me and
him the truth. And he hardly spoke to me again.'

Is there collegiality in the ranks of the players?

'In amateur golf, yes. But pro golf is very, very individi
wouldn't say it's a bitter sport, but it should be called a bitter s
Like, "You're taking my money if you beat me. No matter how
of a friend I am of yours, you're taking away my living, so I've g
beat you if I can" – and if I don't have that inside me . . . I alway
very good on match play, head to head, because I wanted to bea
other guy so bad. Where that came from I've no idea.'

From a small farm in the West of Ireland?

'I played with him twice. I grew to know him and his wife,
Barbara, very, very well, stayed with them when I was in America.
Being friends with the greatest golfer in the world was a real bonus.'

So, apart from mind, heart and stomach, what else does Nicklaus
have that others don't?

'Courage – you can't buy that one, you're born with that. It's a
thing that comes from family. Long, drawn-out thing. And Christy
Senior has it. Luckily I think I had a bit of it.'

Only a bit of it?

'A fair bit of it. Yeah.' He laughs. He has a terrific laugh, a chortle
that his torso takes on board, then distributes to the rest of the body.

He stops, becomes serious. Courage may be innate but 'you still
have to express it. Make it work for you rather than against you. I've
seen great players out there and when you turn on the light, they just
go. Unfortunately. It's terrible to see those great golfers go like that.
There is a type of nervousness that helps rather than hinders you.'

Adrenalin?

'Yes, but you have to be able to control it. If you're too cocky, you
throw it.'

He wouldn't be a great fan, now, of the current fad for mental
conditioning and training. 'No, I never did that. Nowadays, of course,
it's a different game.'

He had his own methods, learned at the knee of You Know Who:
'My uncle taught me lots of stuff in my time. Inner chat is wonderful.
Talking to yourself inside. When you're down and when you're
behind or whatever, the best chat is what you tell yourself inside.
Believing in yourself and telling yourself to "Go!", because even with
just a few holes ahead it can make a big difference. They can drop a
few shots, you can pick up a few shots – there's a huge balance there.'

Can he explain what it's like to be neck and neck coming towards
the last two greens, when the guy you're playing is tracking you shot

by shot, as happened in the joust between hi
at the Belfry when our Christy got the bett
one with The Shot on to the eighteenth gree
golfers – honestly!)

'That can be off-putting. Because what you
play and that's not good. You should never p
should play the golf course at all times. What
beating the course better than he's beating it
better than he does, you win. Simple as that.'

You're not watching him? Playing mental
him?

'Sure you'
happen ing arc
are, and you
trouble or you
close to the pi
chance to get c
not stopping y
he's not holdin
chance too.'

Before we g
to know what
you're so close

Turns out t
going into the
whatever – is n
can happen. 'Th
the cut. If you'r
go home. And
family . . .

'Usually you

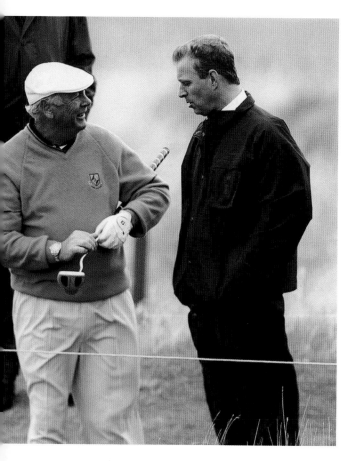

'I know you like it but you can't have it.' Christy with Prince Andrew, Wales Senior Open, 2002.

'I dunno. If you listen to the old pros, "If you're one up you must go two, if you're two up you must go three," and so on. That's the way I played match play. I never settled for being one up, pick them off as quickly as possible.'

It's called a killer instinct, Christy.

And this is why, for most professional players, a team event such as the Ryder Cup is good, fine, brilliant and all that, 'and it was very, very lovely to be in the right place at the right time, but winning an individual tournament – there's something about that. You're on your own from day one.' You're proving to yourself, your harshest critic, that you can still do it.

O'Connor cannot cage this competitive spirit, 'even against my kids, whether it's pool or darts or shooting. Even playing them at golf, and giving them their shots or whatever, I would do everything in my power to beat them. It's a terrible thing. And I used to hear my wife going, "For God's sake, will you stop!" But I couldn't. And I suppose that's incomprehensible to a mother. But it's nothing to do with gender. You have no chance at pro golf if you're not that way.'

There is one exception to this all-consuming competitive streak, of course. It's Guess Who. 'I treat him as something completely different. He's just up there.'

My Deep Throat, the one who helped me with the nine-holes-for-four-rounds stuff, tells me that in the pro-am competitions, when you'd have Tiger, or Christy, or Padraig playing some guy whose day job is staring at a computer screen or working a calculator, the will to win in the heart of the pro is just as fierce. 'You'd have people saying, "Ah, for God's sake, why wouldn't he just pop one in the water? Let the poor guy win." But they never do.'

He does have very strong back-up for this driving and striving, does Christy: 'Himself' always in the background; his second son, Nigel, a solicitor and no mean golfer himself, acts as his legal adviser,

while his daughter, Ann, runs his business. Christy's wife, also Ann, has been with him throughout. 'Everybody, every pro, admires her. She was born with it. She followed me every competition, rain, hail, snow, every tournament, racing back to the kids. That was a huge thing to have in my life. Years ago, when I was practising, she would finish work at five, she was a nurse, and she would follow the balls

Overcome: Christy with wife Ann and Ryder captain Tony Jacklin

for me until ten at night. Collect them and bring them back to me.'

The support was 'unconditional. It didn't matter where I finished. I've seen guys [after a poor result] with their wives going, "What the hell's wrong? What happened? We've a house, we've kids." Ann knew what she was getting into before she got married. We went out together for years before we did, when I was winning just little Irish tournaments. And, yes . . . She knew . . . She was there for everything.'

All right, calm down, golfers. We're at The Shot. At last.

'The Shot, as most people don't recognise, didn't start there. It started at the beginning of the season. To get on the Ryder Cup team is a bloody tough job. You have to be one of the top twelve in Europe. That's a very, very hard battle, particularly coming down to the end of it if you're from tenth position upwards, and I always was in those last three spots and trying to hold on.'

What's the criterion for selection?

'Work I suppose. Practise for every tournament. And you don't take weeks off. You probably should, because you wear yourself out. I eventually got there anyway and got chosen for the team – that was the biggest part.

'The great thing you carry with you into the Ryder Cup team is you're actually playing fantastic golf. So you have to keep reminding yourself, Remember how you got here.' Inner chat.

He did suffer 'a bit of a dart' when he found that Tony Jacklin, the captain, had chosen him to play Fred Couples. 'He [Jacklin] must have thought something of me to put me in that position.'

Jacklin had probably been watching O'Connor's form. 'I had played with Ballasteros in the practice rounds and Seve said to me, "I wish to God I was playing as good as you." Coming from him, that meant something! And my uncle was following me around and he's saying, "Jeekers, I never seen you playing like this before – you're very confident."'

So the fact of being chosen for the team upped his game?

'Absolutely! It had certainly upped my confidence.'

The match began. And here it is, golfers, his own words, exactly the way he tells it.

'We started off and there was never more than one hole between us. I was either one up, one down or all square with Fred, the whole way.

'On seventeen, I hit a fantastic two iron that nobody saw. And that was the makings of the two iron on the eighteenth.

'That two iron on the seventeenth was two hundred and sixty-six yards, which is a long way for a two iron, but the ground was quite running on that particular hole – it's very firm in front of the green. I knew I couldn't carry it all the way. I knew if it bounced good it would run the rest. Which it did.

'And that was huge . . .

'Tony Jacklin had been watching from a hill, one of the mounds, not far away, with the vice captain, Bernard Gallagher. And they were saying, "What the hell's this guy at with a two iron?" They knew I wouldn't be the longest hitter – I'd be middle of the road. But I'd felt sure that if I could carry it two hundred and twenty yards, the ground would take it forward. And it did. We'd read it right. My caddy was very, very good that day.

'Matthew Byrne . . .

'Now, when we came to the eighteenth, I wanted to hit a five wood. Because it was an easier club to hit with, I felt, but it's not as easy to hit it straight. And I said: "Matthew, this is a five wood."

'"No way!" he said. "This is a two iron. You're after hitting the best two iron shot of your career and this is a two iron choice."

'There was water in front. To run off the tee with water in front you have to get in position, which I had, thank God. But now I have this huge expanse of water to carry again, and two hundred and thirty-one yards to get to the pin. "No," he said to me again. "This

is a perfect two iron for you."

'There was hardly any grass on it and I love that, because coming from a sandy area, practising all my life where you wouldn't have too much grass, you hit down on the ball.

'And I said, "Are you certain?"

'And he said, "Absolutely! Two iron."

'One of the things any golfer will do when you go tight is, you don't turn on the back swing, you shorten. And that's lethal. And I remembered that morning one of the things my uncle had said: "Whatever you do, if you can, if you're going to be able, it's not going to be easy, make sure you make a full shoulder turn."

'It's the one thing I thought about. "For God's sake," I said to myself, "you get back!" It's easier said than done because you get faster whether you like it or not with your swing.

'And I'm looking at the back of the green and it's like forty or fifty thousand people, and it's absolutely, like, I dunno, a hundred thick.

'And I hit this shot. I couldn't believe it. I knew by the sound.

'And thank God I didn't see any drips coming up out of the water.

'And it pitched . . .

'Now, I never knew it was going to finish up where it did. There were three tiers on the green. I knew by the flight of the ball that it would hit one of them. That it was going to stop.

'I got it perfect on line. Never left there and finished three and a half feet from the hole.

'And I knew that Freddie, who had out-driven me by quite a long way – he was quite long and deep – I knew that he was frozen. He could not believe – because I had had such a distance to go – that I would even hit the green. He had hit such a fantastic drive. Incredibly long, so hugely long. I mean, massive. Under pressure you do that too.

'He never thought I was going to give him such a run. He was number one in the world. He probably thought he'd beat me three

Opposite and overleaf: Christy triumphs! Fred Couples congratulates him.

and two, or four and three.

'I think when I hit that shot he looked back at me. And I think he went cold.

'And that's why he hit that shot. Like, from where he was he should have hit the green, but he missed it and landed five metres to the right. Had a very difficult pitch, up and down to get on the green – two shots to get out of there. There's a huge slope on the green, you see. And he didn't get up and down, chipped in and missed the putt. So that left me with two.'

O'Connor is sitting away from the back of his seat. He's reliving those moments so vividly he has me living them with him. I can see it all, the crowds, Freddie, the sky above, the emerald grass; I can even smell the sweat and I know I shouldn't interrupt at this crucial juncture, but the event is so amazing, the way he's looking at those crowds, that green, Freddie's disappointment, I have to join in: And you knew you had it?

'I had it then. It wasn't that I'd made him hit a bad shot, I just froze him.

'Two putts from that distance of three and a half feet to win. And I didn't have to.'

We both sit back to take a breath.

'It's in every single country in the world now.'

What is?

A photograph of the full swing. 'I think they made about two thousand prints. No matter what pub I go into. It's lovely, some little pub, some little old pub, I go in and it's there.

'I have a fantastic plaque in the ground there at the spot. Bronze. And they give you a mat, a tiny little mat, twelve inches square. Outings are run to this plaque from beside which, standing on their little mats, everyone tries to emulate what I did.'

My favourite yarn concerns the club that hit The Shot that flew around the world.

Christy Junior donated his fateful two iron to a charity auction where it was bought for fifty thousand pounds. Its buyer promptly gave it back to him and he continued using it for play. In 1990, however, his car and contents, including the club, were stolen. (The car was retrieved but at the time of writing, July 2008, that club is still missing. Probably in action.)

Later that year in Kenya, having won that nation's Open, our golfer was in fine celebratory form at the party afterwards. He was approached by an Irish missionary nun who, as nuns will, asked if he would consider donating the famous two iron for her cause.

O'Connor explained regretfully why that would not be possible.

The nun thought for a minute or two and then smiled. 'Who'll know?'

Planes and Sails and Budget Tails

I Do Like to Be Beside the Seaside – with Gillian Bowler

The Budget Bum,
1991

Leave it to the nuns. I firmly believe that, in the leanest of times, the doughty cadre of Irish mothers provincial and sisters superior, numbers dwindling these days unfortunately, displayed such canny business acumen over the years that they could have run multi-national corporations. And, in the case of many missionary orders, they did.

And while there may not have been many among the group who would, overtly at least, approve of some of the marketing tactics employed by some of our current entrepreneurs, I'm willing to bet that in the secrecy of their hearts they would have admired the chutzpah of Budget Travel in plastering the Budget Bum all over our bus shelters.

Do you remember that Budget Bum? The back-view poster of a girl who, with traces of sand on the tanned cheeks blooming on both

Where's a budget bum when you need one? Michael O'Leary announces Ryanair's winter sale, 2004.

sides of her thong, carried a surfboard through a sparkling sea? In the shiny Budget Travel world, with its hot signature colours of red, blue and yellow, neither the Bum nor its owner had a care in the world: Can't wait to get in, the water's great . . .

Red, blue and yellow have always been the predominant colours of travel brochures, but somehow in the seventies and eighties those of Gillian Bowler's Budget did seem to scoop the others. Her girls seemed to be having more fun, her young men were more handsome, her brochure text was more amusing – and informative – her promises were more exciting.

And so, in your bus shelter, saturated and shivering, you huddled against that glorious bottom in an effort to cod yourself that some of the heat and sunshine in which it frolicked might rub off on you. You vowed that in your lunchtime you would hie yourself to the bustling offices of Budget and put down a deposit. The hell with saving. What were overdrafts for, exactly?

We owe a huge debt to Tony Ryan and Michael O'Leary for Ryanair and, before that company's full flowering, to Budget Travel. It was largely due to both companies that, over a short number of years, holiday travel morphed from white gloves, good suits and full board with set meals, to trainers, tracksuits and Holidays for All.

It is a calm, warm and greyish day in May. Gillian Bowler and I are in the living room of the Dublin house, set in a lush, tranquil garden complete with fishpond, that she shares with her husband. Harry pops in and out; Toby, their sturdy black Labrador, chews his pig's ear and thumps his tail in an attempt to catch the eye of his mistress, who today is clad from head to toe in flowing black: she has several formal meetings later.

The story of Gillian's founding Budget Travel at the age of eighteen with just a hundred pounds is famous in Ireland. Within the trade it is also widely accepted that she and Harry Sydner, her business and life partner, make a formidable good-cop bad-cop team: he, clever, tenacious, witty and hard-nosed, she, charming, gracious and supremely camera-friendly but equally clever when it comes to business.

She came to Ireland for the first time as a seventeen-year-old but very senior employee of the London-based company Greek Island Holidays. At the time she enlisted with it at the age of sixteen she became the third member of a three-person operation and, tender age notwithstanding, quickly expanded her job so that she was drawing up contracts, some with airlines involving millions of pounds sterling. 'When they [the founders of the company] discovered I could do it, they went out to do other things – enjoy lengthy holidays, if the truth be told! No mobile phones. They were away – they were away. It was

"Get on with it, just do it, fix it." You had no option. Anything that happened [which in her case, that first year, included an airline strike] you just dealt with it. You get a reputation then that you're able to fix things and you get given more and more to do.'

At seventeen, she was sent to open a branch office in Manchester, 'and, actually, Manchester went on to become very successful, employing up to thirty people. And then they said, "Go to Dublin."'

She did, for three months, repeating the winning Manchester formula to establish a Greek Island Holidays office here. And it was as a new member of the intimate, clubby travel trade in Dublin during this three-month period that she met Harry.

Having returned to London she became 'disenchanted' with her job and the behaviour she perceived within the expanded echelons of Greek Island Holidays. 'Now there were a hundred people working in head office and it had become one of those places where it was getting a bit phoney and people were not doing their jobs and were sucking up to the bosses – classic organisational behaviour.' Said with the hindsight of a person who has chaired several Irish companies and institutions and is a director of more.

She quit and, brimful of confidence that she would get a job in the travel business, came to Ireland to be with Harry.

But within two hours of starting work at a Dublin travel agency, she walked out. 'I had failed to recognise that in those days the differences between Dublin and London were huge. In London it didn't matter what age you were or what your qualifications. It didn't matter whether you were male or female . . .'

Dublin was run differently. Bosses knew best. Men knew best. She was not even a proper woman, for God's sake, but a slip of a girl with not a bit of paper to her name. 'I hadn't realised that Dublin was so far behind in the matter of opportunities for women. You were allowed to make the tea.'

This was not part of the plan, so Gillian walked and shortly thereafter, with a partner (whom she is reluctant to involve in this story because they parted after only three months: 'We had different aims in mind'), set up Budget Travel in a tiny office on Baggot Street with that hundred pounds. Wisely, she started very small and specialised in what she knew: a single destination, Greece. Flights to Athens but with access to Crete, Rhodes and the smaller islands. 'The office rent was paid in arrears, which was the only thing that allowed us to do it.'

Business was not great during that first year, 'just a couple of hundred customers', but when those holidaymakers returned home, they were happy campers. 'All types and various, old ladies going off to a gay island called Mykonos and coming back and telling us they had a great time.'

As Irish people know, Dublin is a village and Ireland is a small town. 'If you're selling anything you have to be very careful – one bad experience will reach twelve or fifteen people; one good experience will reach one or two.'

Budget's pioneer clients talked. They told their friends and families about this lovely new girl in this refreshing new agency that was doing things differently, so that the following year the friends and families tried it for themselves. 'We did slightly better, a couple of thousand. And every year it got slightly better and we did slightly more . . .'

Her timing at start-up had been good. In the seventies, Greece was a novel destination here, whereas in London 'going to Greece was the most fashionable thing you could do. Where I'd lived, all the heads of the advertising agencies took a rucksack, two pairs of shorts and two T-shirts and went backpacking around the islands, despite the fact that they were millionaires. It was the craze, the trend of the time.'

In addition, travel agents in Dublin would not sell double rooms to single people 'unless they paid extra for the modesty screens'.

The wha'?

'It's true. I don't know whether they were actually called that but I do know that people had to pay extra for a screen.'

So with beauty, brains, experience, nous and an open policy on modesty screens, this upstart chick with the sunglasses on her head and the winning ways began making waves in the travel business. She was born media-savvy and 'The big net gain for me was that all the newspapers were writing about me because I was so different. It meant I didn't need any money for advertising or marketing in the early days and gradually people like Joe Walsh Tours and Bray Travel were asking themselves, "How's she doing it? She's getting to be a difficulty. She's getting to be a player." They hadn't realised it in the beginning.

'We were very conscious of being different. When you went to Greece with us, you saw all the girls wearing thongs and running down the beach without their tops on.' So Irish girls threw off their tops too, even straightened their shoulders to pose for a passing cameraman. But then – omigod – he was pulling out his notebook and pencil. And he's going, "What's your name, luv?" No way, José! "Oh, Jesus Mary and Joseph, you can't put my name in, no way! My mammy would kill me!"

'In those days, all our customers cared about was whether their mammies or aunties knew what they were up to. There was such a tussle going on in Ireland at that time. You grew up, you got married, you settled down. Women didn't continue in careers because of the marriage bar. The height of glamour was to be an Aer Lingus hostess and, without being rude, it's kind of hard to conceive how wheeling trolleys up and down and serving people drinks could be perceived as glamorous . . .'

The typical Budget client, on the other hand, was to the forefront of the gradual move into 'what had already happened in Britain –

'Old ladies going off to a gay island called Mykonos and coming back telling us they had a great time.'

freedom. Our brochures were meant to reflect that.'

Budget's brochures, which included been-there-done-that maps and restaurant reviews, moved goalposts, especially with their unusually honest descriptions of accommodation. 'This place, frankly, is the cheapest place you're going to get. It has a bed . . .' – 'I don't think we used the word "dump". At least, not exactly.'

By the time Bray Travel went bust in 1980, Budget had a client roster of between thirteen and fifteen thousand people every year. It was time for a further step. 'I was the first one to get a bond [to guarantee clients' funds] – we used it as a dramatic publicity exercise.'

The elders of the trade were not best pleased with yet another march being stolen. Joe Walsh personally lifted the phone to unleash a tirade that, seasoned with invective, let Budget's principal know exactly what he thought of her and her publicity-seeking: '"And we know you only got the first one because it was numbered 001. It's not because you're any better than the rest of us!" He hated me always. But a couple of weeks before he died, he made peace.' He rang her out of the blue: 'Can we have coffee? I'm sorry for the things I said.' Their rapprochement is still a source of gladness to her.

During those years, as Budget went from strength to strength, we became accustomed to seeing Gillian – and thinking of her – as the epitome of sophistication and success as, with sunglasses safely anchored in her dark hair, she was greeted by Gay Byrne on *The Late Late Show* to tell us about what she had in store for us this season. Does she remember the moment when she knew she had cracked it?

The answer is surprising. Never. Repeated with vehemence: 'Never!'

We didn't see it from her side because she made sure we didn't. For instance, I attended a few of the now legendary annual parties held for the launches of the Budget brochures, rollicking through the melee of other journalists and liggers, many of whom were as far removed from travel, or even business coverage, as my toenail is from Antarctica.

Those bashes, held in Dobbins restaurant and bedecked with sunny beach paraphernalia, were lavish, offering slap-up food, enough drink to float Noah's Ark, raffles for travel vouchers and holidays. Admission required no introductions, credentials or even intent to publish. Yet this was in an era when journalists were not yet jaded, so that Gillian, a serene and charming happy-ever-after princess in stylish clothes, with heels high, lashes long and manicure perfect, could work the room in the certainty of favourable column inches over the following days and weeks. 'In those days we were creating a form of goodwill towards Budget Travel. We lived in a society then where the only way to get your name out was through the media.

'It was all about perception. For eight thousand pounds, you buy a second-hand car that looks flashy, where a new Nissan something-or-other would cost twenty – and everybody says, "Oh, you've got loads of money because you've got a sports car!"'

The reality was seriously different. 'It wasn't a lovely fairytale. It was continuous worry. We were up to our eyes in debt. Every day was spent talking to the bank manager in a state of almost continual flashes of "Where're we going to get the money to pay people?"' With no backers or bank funds, and highly conscious of obligations not only to customers but to Budget's staff, the owner of Budget Travel spent every morning and afternoon of every working day 'doing cash-flow projections as well as the finances and running the business. It's all very well to talk now about how tough it was. If I'd talked then, Lombard and Ulster wouldn't have loaned me money at twenty-three per cent per annum, which was one of the rates of interest going at the time.'

How quickly we have forgotten. These days, we are resentful when the European Central Bank decides to raise its base interest rate from four to 4.25 per cent – or, perish the thought, even higher. Do you remember paying 22.25 per cent interest on your mortgage? I do. That was when the dinner specials in my house were mince stew, omelettes, sausages-and-mash or 'Mammy's Surprise' constructed from leftovers. Though the only people depending on me were my famly.

For people like Bowler, 'you don't get the rewards without putting in the risk, nevertheless– it's the basic tenet of business. You hide the pain in the formative years because you're out there selling yourself and playing happy face.' Even when Harry left his own travel business in 1982 to join forces with her in running Budget and when, in the public and society page view, everything was tickety-boo, 'until it came around to the time of selling it, I didn't know that we did have a business that had been worth it all'.

"It all", in business terms, is like motherhood: the whole of life. 'It's synchronous. You can't divide your life up. When you're working for yourself you really do work and think business for every waking hour seven days a week. I don't know how nowadays people can say they're going to take two weeks off and go into a retreat and achieve Zen-like calm. I hear around town that you get people interviewing for top jobs and they say in the interviews how important it is to them to get the work–life balance right.'

She doesn't go for that? For diaries colour-coded green for family time, orange for health time, red for work and so on? No?

'I have to be honest. You have to work your backside off. I agree that it's great to take your seven-year-old out to play football and it's great to be able to take a week off here and a week off there because you want to be with your family, but in terms of what a business needs, it needs blood, sweat and tears from you seven days a week. It doesn't stop. If you're at the upper levels of management, if you're a chief executive, you've got to be available seven days a week. You've got to be able to jump on a plane and respond to something unexpected. That includes if you're going on holiday with your family. Some crisis occurs, all the chief executives I know in all the major firms would say to their families, "I'm sorry." You give your life to the business. There's no division.'

Let's get back to the Budget Bum, the appearance of which was the sensation *du jour* during part of that snowy January in the early eighties. The concept was born in conversations between Harry and Tom Banahan, who was the creative director of the company's advertising agency. Yet initially, they felt Ireland was not yet ready.

The photo was a library shot – Gillian thinks it was taken in Australia – but the bosses in the ad agency were iffy on being shown the proof. In fact, with guns sheathed, the two honchos had come trailing back to the office to announce: 'We have to come up with something better.'

'Show me,' Gillian demanded.

They did.

'It's great. What are you talking about?'

'But women will complain!'

'Well I'm a woman and I'm not complaining!'

Tom and Harry considered this. Then, tentatively, from Tom: '"I suppose we could touch it up? Paint on more of a bikini?"'

But Gillian had made up her mind. No bikinis. The poster stood.

They organised a month-long sales campaign, slapping copies of the poster on to billboards and bus shelters. 'We certainly had intended there to be a reaction. We had hoped for a reaction.'

They waited.

And waited.

Nothing happened. The sophistication and open-mindedness of the Irish people had apparently outpaced their judgement of it, 'and we thought, Well, there was no point in doing that!'

They were so desperate 'we were discussing whether to call into the radio shows ourselves to complain' when, ten days before the campaign was due to finish, salvation took an unlikely form. The *Irish Times* published a photograph of children throwing snowballs. The hook was that they were throwing these snowballs right in front of the hot Budget Bum poster. Heat and cold. Yin and yang. The contrast shot, always a winner.

Well, the law of unintended consequences kicked in and, on behalf of the innocent children who could be corrupted by the presence of such filth, Mesdames and Messieurs de Farges got busy with their outraged dialling fingers and quill pens. Gerry Ryan did an 'Are ya for or against the Budget Bum?' survey (in which 85 per cent voted for) and even the august John Bowman took a question about it on *Questions and Answers*. 'Des O'Malley was on the panel. He did a very stiff-upper-lip thing: "She's a very astute businesswoman and she knows exactly what she's doing and we're here talking about it on this show, which is exactly what she wants us to do."'

She laughs. 'Very true . . .'

During the consequent interviews, Gillian had to defend the poster's use in bus shelters against the accusation that when women were standing beside it late at night, they might feel threatened. 'I did think there might be some validity in that.'

Women, however, responded to this and said they felt grand, thank you very much. Not threatened at all.

Despite Gerry Ryan's survey, the company was ordered by the powers-that-be to take the thing down but instead cheekily slapped a sticker across the bum ('Don't Get Left Behind!') It was mischievous, high risk, but it worked. 'We got a second wave of publicity,' and a surge in the company's fortunes. 'Afterwards our ad agency said that a twenty-thousand-pound campaign achieved coverage worth a million and a quarter.' It also ran the Budget Bum into Irish advertising history.

They did try follow-up campaigns ('Jesus, Mary and Joseph –

Great Family Holidays; Repent All Ye Sunners') but ran into more trouble, more complaints to the Advertising Standards people. So, as they had made their splash and things were humming, they decided not to go looking for trouble (are ya listening, Michael O'Leary?) and reverted to the colourful-but-ordinary.

I ask her if she misses the buzz surrounding the start-up phase of a business, the anticipation, the enthusiasm . . .

Bad question.

'The great buzz about start-ups is in other people's minds. All the figures tell you that you're seventy per cent likely to go bust in the first year, maybe eighty per cent, and that goes down slightly in the second year. Those figures aren't dreamed up.'

She does acknowledge that there were some thrilling aspects to the emergence and ascent of Budget Travel. 'What was great was the collegiality and the spirit of the people who worked there when it got a bit bigger. They were as proud of our success as we were on the surface.' Even within the company, however, there remained the element of legerdemain. 'They had no idea that paddling away underneath were the financial problems that we were trying to deal with.'

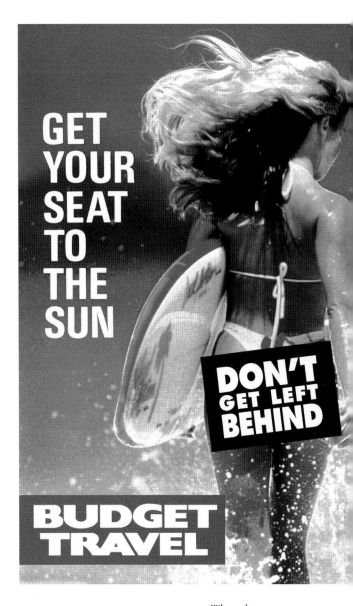

What a bummer.

She denies she was born with a talent to organise. 'Don't give me an original sheet of paper because I will lose it. It used to be the case that anybody who worked with me always took a photocopy of everything. I always delegate those boring things to other people.'

Instinct and common sense is the way to go. 'At the moment, it's all business models and consultants' reports and spreadsheets but sometimes you have to ask the brutal question, "Is this a good idea?" Hey, look here, we've got a great new product, it's like Coke with the bubbles taken out – but does anyone really want to buy flat Coke? I know I sound like a killjoy but people come up with business ideas all the time. People who have been through economics courses and Bachelor of Science courses. They've gone to lectures in various universities but they haven't actually gone and done what people need to do, which is to find something that people actually want to buy.'

In 1987, Gill and Harry sold Budget Travel to the giant British Granada. Not being Irish, with the Irish penchant for personal financial secrecy, she does not mind people knowing that the price was four 'and a bit' million pounds sterling. 'People can look it up if they really want to.'

They learned greatly from working with a multi-strung organisation of that size, 'largely free from capital restraints. If in Budget we needed five hundred grand to do something, well, we didn't have five hundred grand so we had to source the finance and that took up an awful lot of time and energy. Here all of a sudden you had an owner who said, "I'll give you the money."'

On behalf of Granada, they bought Aer Lingus Holidays, 'which turned out to be a brilliant move. We doubled our market penetration within two years and profits were quadrupling every year. Then Granada did a deal that gave us back ten per cent of the company to stay on [as board members and managers] and in the meantime they made us directors of lots of other companies.'

For instance, they chaired Spring Grove laundries in Dublin and were on the board of Granada Motorway Service Stations in Britain. 'I learned [she's enjoying this] that if you make a sausage longer and you make a cup bigger, but put more ice in the cups and more cereal in the sausage, people think they're getting a much bigger deal and actually, you make a lot more money.'

As a result of their stint with Granada and its subsidiaries, she and Harry, in their own view, became more professional. 'When you're working for yourself you don't fully understand corporate needs. If you were sitting around the Budget board table discussing ideas and innovation the language would be loose to say the least, and rowdy, and somebody would tell a joke in the middle of it. Whereas in a boardroom in London it's very serious and very quiet and "Have you looked at the return on capital, have you done this, or that?" You train yourself into being a much more professional manager.'

Now, while serving on many boards, Gillian finds she is once again spending most of her business life wrestling with finance. This time, however, it is on a vastly larger scale as managing director of Irish Life and Permanent. In common with the leaders of all banks around the world, large and small, she leads her company through difficulties presented by the global credit crunch. She is positive about the eventual outcome, 'eventual' being the operative word.

In the general Irish world, however, she does have a problem with the culture of blame, now seemingly endemic. For instance, 'with health in Ireland, the people on the front line are standing in a fairly indefensible position. When confronted with "My mother's been on a trolley for sixty hours and she's lying in her own faeces", it's "Well, don't blame me, blame Mary Harney!" That isn't going to help anybody in the medium term. We have to learn to deal with shortcomings in a service whether created by you or not by you.'

*Gillian at the Irish
Life and Permanent
news conference
2006.*

On a personal basis, she is resigned to the public reality that, over the years, the adjective 'beauteous', frequently applied to her in the newspaper columns, has shifted towards 'glamorous'. 'I used to say I'd absolutely queue up for plastic surgery. I used to think it's a great thing if it makes you feel better. But now I've changed my mind. I look now at the waxy sheen on women who used to look much better with their wrinkles. Women with faces stretched and immobile, faces I wouldn't want for love or money.'

And yet, she, queen of the brave face, has recently discovered (alarmingly!) that personal appearance does matter even in the most unusual settings. Formal board performance evaluations at one of the institutions of which she is a director have revealed that the get-up and grooming of individual board members does matter to those who share lifts with them. 'It matters quite a lot.'

Dear God . . . What an appalling vista . . .

Wonder what the Budget Bum looks like, these days?

Yowsa! Yowsa! Tourist interrupting!

The Liveliest Mike

Such sunny memories of those magnificent Budget parties in Dobbins.

Twenty years ago, when Mike Murphy was broadcasting daily on daytime radio, he said in an interview we did together in the same restaurant that one of the greatest thrills of his working day was 'to walk past the nest of desks that houses the stressed and worried folk in real programmes. To drift down to studio three or five, past the other studios where there are real recordings of arts and drama programmes in progress. I send them all up rotten. I know they all think I'm a trivial idiot. It's great! I really enjoy being underestimated.'

As youngsters, we were both brought up in an era where, in general, 'work' was grimly what you did outside your real life. But Murphy's innately sunny nature was nurtured by a far-seeing mother who never gave him a hard time about his academic shortcomings: 'Do what you want to do. God made a beautiful, wonderful world, and it's your duty to see as much of it as you can.'

He took her at her word, and nobody is underestimating him now. Reincarnated as a businessman and successful property developer, he spins between the US, the Bahamas and Ireland as an executive director for Harcourt Developments. He lives a lot of the time in Florida and believes firmly that the waters have closed over his reputation as a broadcaster. 'Look, I know that I'm largely forgotten. I knew my time had come, it was time to go and it was time to let younger people in. Gone but not forgotten. Unlike Gay, forgotten but not gone!'

They are pals. It's a running gag between them.

He sits back in his big director's chair behind his substantial – and cluttered – desk in his office at Harcourt Developments, the company behind Park West and many large sites both here and abroad. The words 'big', 'large' and 'substantial' are apt when used to describe his presence still. In his youth he was a rugby player for his school, Terenure College, and despite some health knock-backs, he retains an aura of physical power and confidence. Only a man of size and substance – and some impudence – could carry off such a pale and sunny outfit on a dank, windy day in Dublin.

'Did the nation go into mourning when I slipped away into the night? Not . . . at . . . all . . .'

'Did my departure make any difference at all to RTÉ? Did it make a difference to anybody? Not the slightest.' One of Murphy's defining personality traits is a conundrum. He has made an art of witty self-deprecation, but in truth this is ironic, a declaration of his own abilities. Before 'rolling news', a.k.a. *Morning Ireland*, was conceived, who remembers surfing towards the working day on the waves of good humour emanating through kitchen and car radios from the

Our hero in business mode with Bertie and Pat Doherty at the official opening of Park West, October, 1999.

presenter of *Morning Call?*

A personal survey, conducted by me on my own behalf, reveals that most people over a certain age remember the faint 'Yowsa! Yowsa!' that, for seven years in the late seventies, bubbled every now and then into the morning cornucopia of music, news, listeners' letters and chat over which Murphy presided. It was the herald of and sometimes understated accompaniment to a programme segment instituted by Murphy and his producer, Gene Martin: the 'Rotten Record'. They used it, I suspect, primarily to entertain themselves, but comfortable in the knowledge that collateral enjoyment would arise for the listeners. One of their regulars was a ditty from the ballsy but execrable singer, Mrs Miller. 'Her "Downtown" was a classic. So nearly in tune but not quite.'

Then there was the legendary, and very rich, Florence Foster Jenkins. Mrs Foster Jenkins hired Carnegie Hall and a full professional orchestra to enchant her legions of fans. Recordings of these events are the mainstays of many disc collections because 'she could very nearly sing opera'. Apparently, such was the lady's pulling power that her concerts were sell-outs, her strutting rendition of 'Habanera' from *Carmen* while simultaneously flinging carnations into the audience always eliciting cheers and calls for 'Encore!'

She would oblige, but not before asking the audience if they wouldn't mind returning the carnations. The flinging of them, you

A real book –
The Arts Show,
1989.

see, was an essential part of her performance. So they willingly threw them up and sat back for more.

Murphy and Gene Martin made the perfect iconoclastic team. 'Gene was a good deal older than me but he was so mischievous and such fun and so anti-establishment. Very dapper, very sophisticated. Wicked sense of humour. He could be very bitchy with people, though.'

Indeed he could. 'Gene discovered a little soundbite of a belch. Don't know where he got it. And there was a weather man he didn't like.'

The *Morning Call* studio had access to the main on-air channel, including the conduit to the Met Office.

You see where we're going here?

'So when the man would take a breather, Gene would push the button.'

They did it often. The poor forecaster wouldn't have been aware of the gag, but the whole nation got to hear his unfortunate 'lapses'. Murphy agrees that no one would get away with it now. 'It was juvenile and appalling behaviour.' But there is a glint in his eye.

Then there was the 'Erika' march, which sounded as though a jackbooted army, accompanied by a division of panzers, was on the way to overpower some small nation. The pair used to play that at around eight twenty when, around the country, breakfasts were being rushed to get kids off to school. 'It used to annoy and amuse in equal measure. We didn't realise that it was the anthem of the Hitler Youth Movement until someone told us.' Their concession to the receipt of this information was to reduce the frequency with which 'Erika' was played. A little.

The fun did not end with the conclusion of the programme at nine. 'Every morning we'd leave the premises at nine fifteen and go to the Magnet pub in Pearse Street where we'd have two hot whiskeys and a cheese sandwich. And then we'd go round the art galleries.'

Not for these culture vultures and self-appointed bon viveurs the greasy rashers and tough sausages of the RTÉ canteen breakfast.

All changed utterly now, of course. The old canteen is just a memory triggered by pinching the roll of fat around the midriff and is now the equivalent of a health farm. As an aside, there is a marvellous canteen story about a lady we'll call Mrs A, for many years a stalwart behind the hot-food counter in my own time there. Eamonn Lawlor, the newsreader with the choirboy looks, was her pet.

One day, however, our hero looked down in dismay at his plate and saw his meat and spuds suffering contagion from the watery liquid oozing from his huge heap of undrained peas. 'Aaah, Mrs A!' He held up the plate to show her.

'Sorry, Éamonn, love.' She grabbed it from him and, snatching a tea-towel from where it drooped at her waist, mopped up the offending slime and handed the plate back to him. 'There y'are now!'

During that era, with no substantive competition from commercial stations, '*Morning Call* was by far the most successful morning radio programme RTÉ ever did.' And for those seven years, after each renewed assault on broadcasting good taste, its presenter could, with confidence, exhort the growing commuter car-radio community to '"Look at the fella in the next car and watch him laughing." And I'd know that this would be happening all over the country.'

As for the origin of the 'yowsa' running gag, that clip too was discovered by Gene. If you've ever seen the film *They Shoot Horses, Don't They?* you'll know that during the 1920s and the Great Depression in America couples entered competitive dance marathons wherein they kept going until one or other literally fell into a standing sleep and was thereby eliminated. To keep them moving at regular intervals a man went around with a megaphone through which, as an aid to wakefulness, he intoned, 'Yowsa! Yowsa!'

'Ah, yeah. Disgraceful behaviour but you wouldn't have missed it for the world.'

If it's not fun, we don't do it. That continues to be one of the main drivers of Mike Murphy's career. He recognised this early, unlike so many people who grind through life, postponing fun 'until I have time' and then run out of days. 'I did not enjoy my schooldays. I loved all the ancillary things, the rugby and the sport and all that stuff.'

But in the classroom he was a 'disaster. I ended up in the A class but I was acting my way through, looking intelligent while not having a bog what they were talking about. One side of my brain didn't work – the side for mathematics and science and so on. I didn't even make ten per cent in any of those subjects in my Inter, or in Irish.'

Every morning, particularly on Mondays, he dragged into school 'with a leaden stomach' and has subsequently applied the 'leaden-stomach test' to every move he has made. 'If I was going into anything in radio or television with a leaden tummy I decided, "This is not for you, sunshine!" Once you begin to feel you're not enjoying something you're doing, it's time to make as graceful an exit as possible.'

His exit from school after the failed Inter was, via his motor-dealer father's business contacts, into a drapery company called Crowe-Wilson. After a year of that, he went into th'oil business. No, not with JR. With Castrol as an office boy.

After that, he was taken on by the late Brendan Smith, who ran an acting academy but also had a finger in the producing pie of sponsored programmes on Radio Éireann. His new assistant's job seemed to involve the carrying about of records from place to place, while looking important in the name of 'producing' these programmes. It also involved eating quite a lot of cream buns.

As a perk, Smith allowed him to take acting courses too. Now here was great gas. It even led to parts in various productions. But then, during a scene in *The Rose Tattoo* at the Eblana Theatre in the basement of Busárus (the roar of the greasepaint, the smell of the urinals), he noticed two ladies getting up out of their audience seats

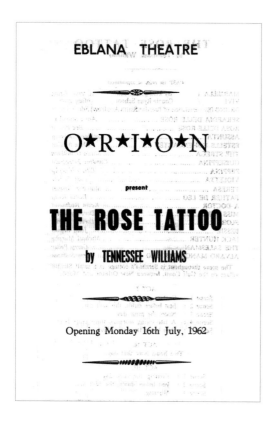

EBLANA THEATRE

O★R★I★O★N

present

THE ROSE TATTOO

by TENNESSEE WILLIAMS

Opening Monday 16th July, 1962

The smell of the greasepaint, the roar of the urinals: programme cover from Mike's mercifully short acting career.

to leave in disgust at the lines he was delivering. He stopped in mid-flow and directed them politely towards the ladies' toilet.

The producer, Phyllis Ryan, was not amused. So acting, perhaps, was not to be his true vocation, after all. He does claim, however, to have plumbed the shallows of the stage: 'If I had stayed at acting, I would have ended up in one of those terribly cheap series as some kind of well-known cad. A grotty series that everybody watched. If I was ambitious, I know I would have set my sights on something as high as *Dallas*.'

So, with acting now in the past tense, he responded to an advertisement for radio announcers in Radio Éireann. And was not chosen. He re-auditioned. And was not chosen. But the late Denis Meehan liked the sound of his voice and sent him for training in the Irish language. The course went well, although apparently he learned just the sounds and not the language.

He was auditioned yet again, this time given a half-page script in Irish to read aloud.

Afterwards, Meehan said that the reading and interpretation had not been at all bad. Had Mr Murphy understood what he had been reading?

Mr Murphy had indeed – it had been an introduction to a football match.

Tactfully, Mr Meehan overlooked the fact that the piece had been part of the oration over Wolfe Tone's grave. 'He said I was close . . .'

In any event, he was taken on as a part-time radio announcer and

Now for something completely different – The Collector.

began the progression in broadcasting that was to lead him right to the top. A progression always characterised by moving onwards and never repeating past glories.

Years later, 'I had done every bloody daytime slot, every kind of format, and most of them had bored the bejaysus out of me, and I decided I couldn't go on any longer. So I said to myself, "Listen, you have run out of clichés," and so I took myself out of mainstream.'

The result was *The Arts Programme* on Radio One, where he was free to learn more about the artistic and cultural goings-on in Ireland from people who knew what they were talking about. He enjoyed it hugely and began seriously to collect visual art, confidence in his own judgement buoyed by those morning perambulations with Gene Martin years earlier.

Television offered opportunities for fun too. After a personal trip to the United States, Murphy approached John McColgan, then a TV producer, with a proposal to film a series there. McColgan ran with it and went to the boss of TV Programmes, who, rather surprisingly, gave the go-ahead. 'All the real producers of documentaries in the station were appalled. These two gobshites going off to the States *with a budget* for six one-hour programmes that they would give their eye-teeth to be doing. Disgraceful use of the station's money.'

But then the programmes, *Mike Murphy's America*, were shown and were a huge success. 'And they were better, I would warrant, than any they would have done.'

He is not in the least overawed by the university set. 'When the impressing starts, there's a lot of "ooh, ye-es" around the table. I have discovered that, mentally, I'm quicker than most and I'm good at assessments.

'At one stage, I did feel I was not intellectually equipped to deal with a number of things, but I don't worry about that any more. As I go through, dealing with them all, I have found that there are not that many of them brighter than I am. In fact, I'm surprised at how naïve they are at many things. I don't understand the jargon, but I don't need to.'

He tried to get RTÉ to let him do a second series of *America* 'but they were entrenched in wanting me on radio on a regular basis and wouldn't let me off'. This was proof, if proof were needed, that Mike's Way was best for Mike's Life – and Mike's Fun. 'I decided never to be pigeonholed again. It's a very easy trap to fall into, fur-lined, but a trap nonetheless. A lot of broadcasters can't wait to be pigeonholed. Have a niche. Then when they're in there, they look around and realise, well, hey! There are other things they'd like to do as well.'

Interestingly, having titled his autobiography *Mike and Me*, he sees the 'Mike' moniker as a construct. 'Mike' is the what'll-he-do-next fella, the mischief-maker, the raconteur and fun guy everyone wants to sit beside at dinner. To family and friends, however, he is Michael. And always will be.

Mike and Michael decided simul- taneously to branch out. 'I see people saying, "Oh God, I'd love to have my own chat show," and I could have had my own on RTÉ but it would have bored me. To me, hosting a chat show is a rather colourless career in one sense – although,' he laughs, 'I'm sure the current incumbents would not agree!'

"Allez les bleus": That *sketch from* The Live Mike.

So, for lack of encouragement to do another series of *Mike Murphy's America*, he conceived *Mike Murphy's Australia*, found the finance and became its executive producer. 'I bullied my way through' and, predictably, 'adored' Australia, its openness, its individualism, its readiness to accept new ideas and a person for who they are, not what they do.

It was in Australia he discerned the first glimmers of a possible change in career. 'All your options are open. I knew I could do well without going near broadcasting and with just business ideas. And I had found the people to go to.'

It was to be a while, though, before he made the leap out of RTÉ.

The fun factor, in front of and behind the cameras, was critical to the concept behind *The Live Mike*, the TV series now famous for its 'Candid Camera' segments involving Murphy himself acting up a storm, wearing disguises – particularly those prosthetic teeth and red wigs – and thoroughly enjoying every minute of his own antics. Remember 'Tourist Interrupting'? The French guy who goaded Gay Byrne into losing his cool? My own favourite from the series is the 'Long Lost Relative' who arrives on the doorstep of a woman in a housing estate to leave in his washing. She has never seen or heard of him before. But she takes it in!

He and John 'Greenbeat' Keogh, his producer for the series, had

wrestled with the philosophical concept of the programme. What would they themselves enjoy? What had been the nicest evening they could remember?

'Good company,' they decided, 'but not an evening of giddy laughter from A to Z. An element of wit, satire – having a go at sacred cows – a good deal of humour, banter, nostalgia, but also some serious conversation where you actually enjoy exchanging ideas with other people.' They threw in a music element and *voilà*! There it was, the perfect format! 'An evening in good company, a good evening out.'

Grand. Great. That was that decided. That would work. Now, who would they like to have with them on such a show? Who would be fun to work with but also terrifically competent and versatile? 'I always believed in surrounding myself with people who are better than me.'

You're a good number two, then?

Oops!

'No, actually, I see myself as a good number one. I know how to handle the people around me even if they're better than me. I'm good at co-ordinating people. Never had the insecurity to believe "Omigod, I can't be outshone." And I never felt jealous either. Maybe I never had the intelligence to feel threatened by other people! Because you're not threatened you can generate loyalty.'

They hand-picked Twink. 'I knew what a good

mimic Twink was. She was very, very versatile. She was known only as a singer at the time, but dying for an opportunity to do something different.'

They decided against professional comedians, 'but I remembered this guy who'd been writing in to *Morning Call*. Funny letters. A lot of them.'

The author of the letters was a teacher in St Michael's, 'who obviously wanted to be in showbiz', and John Keogh discovered that he was performing in UCD. 'So we went over and found this guy doing a send-up of Big Tom. Calling him "Big Gom".' After the show they approached him directly. 'Have you any other characters that you do?'

'Yeah, I have this priest,' replied Dermot Morgan, 'I call him Father Trendy.'

Previous:
The live Mike
looking for his
roots.

The nostalgia quotient, Bridie Gallagher, Rose Brennan, Maisie McDaniel, would be hoicked into the first part of the show. 'And we were getting unlikely people to perform, all kinds of people, Paddy Harte and Glen Barr together . . . Memorably, poor Albert Reynolds singing "Put Your Sweet Lips A Little Closer To The Phone" in a cowboy outfit. He was Minister for Posts and Telegraphs at the time. Nearly killed his career in one go!

'And now we were going to take some difficult sociological issues and we were going to put them right in the middle of the programme.' In this strand they 'followed and filmed a patient undergoing vasectomy'; they 'did' illiteracy in the same manner – 'His employer didn't know the guy was illiterate until he saw the programme and I have to say the employer was subsequently fantastic.' They also 'did' wife-beating. 'We interviewed the guy in his place of work. He spoke of the urges he had, and all the rest of it.

'And, of course, the fun of it for us was not just in front of the camera. We had assembled a sensational team behind. It was like choosing the Magnificent Seven. We all had various and varied outside interests too, so backstage we had a fantastic life. I was interested in art and we began to deal in paintings. We dealt in books. We played the stock market . . .'

The atmosphere in the show's office reflected all of this. It was situated in a gloomy annexe away from the main television building and opposite the office of *The Late Late Show*. The contrast between the atmosphere in both rooms, according to Murphy, could not have been greater. While theirs buzzed with mischief, juvenile practical jokes and even anarchy, that of the *The Late Late Show* 'was like the office of an insurance company'.

They began to challenge their seniors in the ratings, and the first time they made number one over the heads of *The Late Late Show* they hung a provocative banner over its door: 'NUMBER ONE IN THE RATINGS! GOOD LUCK NEXT TIME, GAY!'

The reaction across the way, he says, was a quiet 'Tsk! Tsk! Those people! How vulgar!'

It was the quality of *The Live Mike*'s assembled talent that was responsible, in a way, for its premature demise as the programme's 'talent' began to disperse in search of different challenges. 'I found myself with a new crew and things weren't the same. The mixture didn't work as it used to. It was still successful but the fun had gone out of it for me.'

And we know what happens then, don't we?

No one could have forecast the way it did happen, however. 'I never told anybody, but on the very last night of the third series I announced, live on air, "Well, that was the end of *The Live Mike*. I won't be back next year."'

There were ructions, naturally, because the 'little grey men' as he has characterised those who run RTÉ from behind the safety of their desks, had planned and budgeted for another series.

He was adamant, though: it was again time to move on. 'I was never comfortable with authority. Never liked authority. I just saw it differently. I often use the little mantra: I'd rather the company worked for me than the other way around. I'd like to do the things I want to do and let the company pay for them.

'I'm not impressed by titles. Never wanted one. Even in my business career now, I'm a director of Harcourt Developments but I don't want to be marketing director, or director of operations. I just want to be minister without portfolio. I'm very much of the view that we have a short life span and you should get to do as much as you possibly can do. And test your own capacity to see how well you get on.'

He was always up for a challenge. For programmes, he parachuted out of an aeroplane, was thrown in judo by a twelve-year-old girl, went into a lion's cage with half a dozen lions, 'two of whom had been in a major fight just before I went in. The one who was bleeding was the one that had to jump over my head.'

The failures, few though they were and mostly insignificant, do rankle. Hang-gliding, for instance – to 'failure' he adds the adjective 'abject': 'I resent the fact that I allowed myself to fail. I just lost my nerve. I just couldn't face going off that cliff.' Neither was every broadcasting effort a shining achievement. 'The arts programme I did on TV, Arts Express, was pretty poor. My bits were always left to the last few minutes of recording. I didn't like it and I was very uncomfortable.'

As we get older, despite well-meaning or even new-agey convictions to the contrary, no matter how robust the spirit, the opportunities to try new things do diminish. Murphy acknowledges he will never now be a sports star or an architect – he would have liked to try both – but he accepts he has had 'the most blessed career, twice, in broadcasting and now in business. I've enjoyed every moment of both careers. Given the duration of the natural life one is hoping for, I have been blessed with what I've managed to get done in mine.'

He has been lucky, too, 'but I think to a huge extent a lot of it is making your own luck. And I think courage is a big, big thing in the living of one's life. The courage to take decisions and have faith that something will come around to compensate and "take the place of". I think I have been quite courageous in my life in that I did experiment and change.'

He regrets nothing except, like the rest of us, personal failings, such as not knowing how to be the best parent possible to our children, in his case, four.

His business life has conferred gravitas along with the greying hair, but it's a gravitas easily punctured by delight at the prospect of some new project. His sense of humour and mischief remain undimmed, as does his self-belief. Critically, the shoots of interest in business that he first recognised in Australia have matured.

As for his opinion that he is not publicly missed, he does know of one broadcaster who has let it be known he wants to be 'like Mike Murphy was'. 'He wants to do documentaries and have a more colourful career.'

He understands that impulse, applauds it and is not in the least worried that his unique heritage in Irish broadcasting will be equalled, copied or capped. Doesn't care about that codswallop. He has his bright life in Florida, his business interests there, here and in the Bahamas, attracts growing respect for his business acumen. Broadcasting for him is history, glowing, happy, but gone. 'Everybody is expendable. Nobody will be missed. Only the really great. The Heaneys.'

Rivers of Blue Light

The Stardust

Many Irish people believe that Charlie Bird is not expendable: that no event becomes real unless Charlie Bird is standing there, confirming it for us.

Charlie's phone rang in his Bray home, shortly after one o'clock in the morning on 14 February 1981. 'Mr Radio', as Bird calls Mike Burns, was the man on the other end of the line.

Up to the time he left, anyone who has passed through the newsroom of RTÉ on the radio side of things, will count Mike, bon viveur, possessor of the most extraordinary thatch of strawberry blond hair and scourge of cub reporters who might harbour notions of their own brilliance, as a primary influence in how they did their jobs. The man was and is a legend in broadcasting, adored the diplomatic and political circuits, loved a good cigar. He had the best nose in the business for a good story and was a hard taskmaster:

'good enough' wasn't good enough. 'Charlie,' said Mike now, 'there's been a big fire in North Dublin.'

In his memoir, *This Is Charlie Bird*, the RTÉ newsroom's chief reporter devotes four pages to one of the biggest stories he covered in his early days. The fire at the Stardust nightclub has stayed in his mind as perhaps one of the most significant of his career. Forty-eight young boys and girls were killed that night. Responding to the phone call from Burns, he headed off and, although not really knowing the north side of Dublin, had little difficulty finding his way to the Stardust nightclub. He followed the rivers of pulsing blue lights. And

Outside the City Morgue.

no one in Dublin, or indeed in Ireland, can forget those pictures of white-faced, terrified youngsters pressed against the barred window of a toilet as those outside tried desperately but in vain to pull them to safety, of hospital wards filled with bandaged kids, of the processions of heartbreaking funerals in the succeeding days.

The night had started so promisingly all over Artane and other districts of northside Dublin. Brothers and sisters, sisters and sisters, teasing each other through the closed doors of bathrooms all over the area. The smell of hairspray and affordable perfume was at sneezing level; there was a lot of 'Tell me the truth: do I look fat in this?'

Valentine's Day is the height of life for teenagers and more than eight hundred and forty were crammed into the Stardust's disco area, decorated with a few Valentine folderols in honour of the day. The teenage function was not the only one in the Stardust that night. There was a trade-union do on elsewhere in the complex.

Like many a disaster, it started small and so simply. Someone noticed flames on a couple of seats in a closed-off bar area. Attempts were made to extinguish them but the seats were made of foam and the fire seemed to be spreading. A little.

The trade-unionists were advised to leave – which they did, unscathed – and then security staff tried to raise the shutters to close off the affected area. The flames jumped to the ceiling tiles and spread quickly. Noxious fumes and thick black smoke filled the disco.

The kids panicked and rushed for the marked exits. One proved to be chained and padlocked; two were blocked. Two more, although not locked, had chains draped over them and the youngsters, verging on mass hysteria, assumed that they, too, were barred.

Some dashed into the toilets and climbed over each other to get at the windows. But they found that metal grilles had been welded over the openings.

The alarm had been raised by those who had already escaped and outside, with others, they tried desperately to remove those toilet windows with anything to hand, including tow ropes tied to the backs of cars. Nothing worked.

The personnel riding the first wave of five fire engines and two ambulances, seeing what was going on, called for back-up and for the activation of Dublin's Major Disaster Plan. Eleven Dublin Fire Brigade ambulances, along with those of the Eastern Health Board, began ferrying the injured to the Mater, Jervis Street, Richmond, Doctor Steevens's and St Vincent's hospitals. At Store Street, the army erected tents to ease the overcrowding at the City Morgue, while, at the Stardust, firefighters wearing breathing apparatus found bodies stacked on top of each other at the fire exits. Some had been trampled in the stampede. Some had succumbed to smoke inhalation.

Anecdotal evidence has it that when firemen burst into the men's toilet, where one group was trapped, an older teenager was in the process of assuring the younger ones with him that they would all be in heaven soon. This group was taken safely out.

At approximately one forty-five a.m., the blazing ceiling collapsed and the lights went out, intensifying the panic and hysteria of those still inside.

Meanwhile, those outside, agonised, could still see white faces against immovable bars only inches away and for whom they could do nothing; and when Charlie Bird arrived, his reporter's eye for detail kicked in: it was a very cold night and he remembers that while the fire hoses were being played on what was now an inferno, leaks from the hydrants froze almost immediately to form icicles.

Next day, the Taoiseach, Charles Haughey, in whose constituency the tragedy had occurred, toured the gutted building, and announced that, out of respect for the bereaved, the injured and their families, the Fianna Fáil Ard Fheis was to be cancelled.

An inquiry was held subsequently. Some of its findings – such as that the fire was started deliberately when a cigarette was used to ignite foam-filled seats – are still in dispute, and the subject of ongoing demands by victims and their families for a new inquiry.

Some findings are not in dispute. The Butterlys, owners of the Stardust, were found guilty of negligence. It was revealed that the reason for the locked door and for the grilles welded to the windows of the toilets was to prevent teenagers admitting their pals without payment.

Aftermath.

Two Quadrants of the Night Sky

Disasters at Bantry and Buttevant

At five past one on the morning of 8 January 1979, the telephone rang on the bedside table of Tom McSweeney, RTÉ's ex-Munster correspondent, who was deeply asleep. He and his wife, Kathleen, had been celebrating all weekend: he had had a great leaving party at the broadcasting station on the Friday and was looking forward to starting work on the Monday at NET, the Irish State's fertiliser factory. He was to be paid an annual two and a half thousand pounds more than he had been getting as a newsman. He would have six staff and a company car. Although Kathleen had prophesied that he would not stick the new job as public relations manager, Tom had felt he and his family could not in all conscience let a thirty-eight per cent increase in salary, plus perks, slip by. His dreams were sweet.

The phone rang again. This time he opened one eye. Five past one? It couldn't be! Could it?

It was. 'Hello, Tom, Mike here.'

Mike Burns. Again.

'Hello, Mike?' Tom rubbed the sleep from his second eye. Could it be that Mike was under the illusion that the leaving party was still on? 'What can I do for you?'

'Tom, there's a story in Bantry – we need you to go.'

'Hold on, Mike, I left RTÉ last Friday. I don't work for RTÉ any more.'

'Don't give me that. Go down at once. There's a tanker, there's lots of people dead, get out of bed and go!'

'But, Mike, I haven't even got a tape-recor—'

'Stop giving me that! Will you get out of bed and go? We need you down there. We need you down there now!'

End of conversation. Meekly, the PR manager for NET got out of bed.

Kathleen propped herself up on one elbow. 'Where're you going?'

'I'm going to Bantry, there's a tanker—'

'But you don't work for RTÉ any more.'

'But Mike Burns—'

'Ohh!' She lay down again. 'You'd better go, so!'

That call – should he have still worked for RTÉ – would not have been all that unusual. 'Gulf Oil ran Bantry at the time and there had been several pollution episodes. I remember a news controversy down there, and them telling me that they'd only spilled about two hundred and seventy-five gallons. "Listen," I said, "there's only three hundred gallons in my tank in the back garden – it must be more than that."

And it eventually turned out to be hundreds of thousands of gallons. So yet another Gulf Oil story wouldn't have been too surprising.'

His home in Bishopstown is on the western side of Cork city, and within minutes of leaving it, he saw the red glare on the horizon. 'That would have been forty or forty-five miles away but I could actually see it in the night sky. It's a drive of about an hour and a bit, and as I got nearer and nearer, the sky got redder and redder.

'There's a hill going down into Bantry – it dips down and then it rises again and comes into the town. You could actually see the occasional "pouf" and a rising of smoke and flames into the night sky and hear a sort of a muffled bang. And when I got into Bantry, it was almost surreal, with people standing around in the square, all looking up and out towards Whiddy, two miles out in the bay.'

The Gulf Oil terminal was on the island's western side, so the hump of the land obscured it from the town. Yet there could be no mistaking what was going on out there. As he got out of his car there was another explosion, then an eruption of orange flame, 'like in a furnace, followed by circles of smoke and more flame', shooting high into the sky. The night was clear. But while the moon rode peacefully in one quadrant of the heavens, a second quadrant, over Whiddy, was hellish.

The people looking westward from the square in Bantry (some of whom, he figured, had to have relatives working on that island) were quiet. The general feeling was as though the world had paused in its rotation. 'Nobody had ever dealt with anything like this. There were no services or disaster plans.' A few courageous firemen, he was told, had gone out in a boat very early on, their task being to help the Whiddy staff keep the tank farm cool by constant damping down. (Their heroism probably saved Bantry. None of those tanks exploded.)

Wearing a tie too hastily knotted, there was one Garda in the square, 'old-style uniform, big buckle on the belt'. McSweeney approached him: 'What's happening out there?'

'There's lots dead, there's lots dead,' was all the Garda managed to say before he was interrupted by another boom and a deepening of the red in the sky's second quadrant.

The Bantry Bay Hotel was well known to journalists. If you kept your eyes and ears open in there, news or gossip, political or otherwise, could be picked up from the fishermen, Gardaí, county councillors and locals who frequented it. It was open. McSweeney hurried inside and found 'lots of people sitting silently at the bar. Nobody really knew what to say. Every so often, you'd see the heads turn as there was another bang.'

He left the hotel and went down to the foreshore. 'I wanted to see could I get a boat to take me out to Whiddy.'

'You can't,' he was told bluntly by those supervising.

'There were fishermen, people bringing in boats, people coming off the island – "They're all trying to get into Bantry. We're taking people off the island. We'll be lucky if we don't have to evacuate, get everyone out of Bantry if those tanks go."'

For a reporter cognisant of the tragedy unfolding for individuals and families yet intent on getting the story, this was a most frustrating place to be. Today, with twenty-four-hour news and satellite vans, an event of this magnitude would be fully covered within minutes from the first phone call to any newsroom, not only from the ground but from the air. That night, Ireland's national broadcaster had a single envoy, who wasn't even on the payroll and had no equipment. Armed with only the landline number of his former office he was trying to come to terms with a terrible tragedy, which had happened two miles from where he was standing, and to which there were no first-hand witnesses in Bantry. All he could actually see while he was standing with the group of stunned fishermen and others on that foreshore was the gentle hill of Whiddy Island underneath a roiling sky and knew just two facts for sure: the oil supertanker *Betelgeuse* had exploded; there were many casualties.

So he talked to the authorities, who were able merely to hazard guesses. He talked to the dazed people arriving in little boats who had not yet recovered from their sudden awakening. He and the *Irish Times* southern correspondent, Dick Hogan, who had now arrived on the scene, shared any snippets of information they could find. McSweeney was horrified as a human but helpless as a reporter: 'There's a car crash, four dead, there's a bomb, three dead – but how can I get this across? The size of it? What was unearthly, and still is unearthly in my mind, is that even in the initial stages you knew it was so big, and yet there were no bodies. We were being told there were thirty people in the ship's crew. Then somebody told me thirty-five. I was trying to get my head around what the real figure was, how many would be on the pier during an unloading operation, how many lived on the island, close enough to be affected by the initial explosion.'

The final tally of the dead was fifty-one.

When daylight dawned, 'we were able to get a plane down from Dublin and one from Cork'. Once he actually saw the disaster zone, was it better or worse than he had imagined the night before?

'I was just flummoxed. Nobody in Ireland had ever dealt with an exploding tanker before so there was no reference. I suppose the human thing is that you'd always, at the back of your mind, hope that someone from that crew had got off, or been rescued,' a hope that died when the plane took him over the broken-backed hulk of the tanker, still emitting dense plumes of black smoke.

'Until then, I don't think any of us realised what a fire on an oil tanker really means. Those were terrible pictures. What happened to all the bodies? Some were picked up afterwards, but the great majority of those poor people just vanished off the face of the earth. Where the crew was concerned, there was no recovery possible because they were blown apart and incinerated on board.'

He is honest enough to acknowledge that he felt no grief at the time. The event was too big. 'It was like being a spectator at a movie.' And he continues to regret that he was not 'forceful enough and didn't know the fishermen well enough then to convince them to take me out'.

Grief and sorrow came later, developing slowly as he grasped 'the suddenness of death. I've never seen fifty-one bodies. Most of them were probably asleep and never knew. Never knowing.'

There is another feeling too, very difficult to identify. Even more difficult to articulate.

In recent years, Tom McSweeney's main work has been as presenter and producer of *Seascapes*, 'a maritime programme for this island nation', in the course of which he has become the seaman's friend and advocate. His job has become a vocation and it is probably because of this, and his deep empathy with the minds and lifestyles of those who go to sea, that what happened to the crew of the *Betelgeuse* continues to horrify him.

But there's also his sense that, to the Irish public, their fate didn't seem to matter much. Let's be blunt about this: they were foreigners.

Yes, there were tributes and memorials. Yes, they were included in Masses and prayers, 'but apart from the unfortunate local people who were killed – and no disrespect to those victims or their families – nobody knew who they were, who they had been.

'That grates. They died in a horrible conflagration, but they were nobodies. For example, I still don't know the name of any one of them. It was as though we didn't care whether it was thirty or thirty-five or forty-four of those seamen. We weren't being dismissive or not respecting them – it's just that they weren't real. Even years afterwards, the crew of the *Betelgeuse* were just anonymous seafarers.

'Just.'

Six months after that event, eighteen more seafarers died in the

Dutch sailors form a guard of honour as the coffins of two victims of the Fastnet Yacht Race disaster are carried ashore from the warship Overijssel at Plymouth, 17 August 1979.

Fastnet Race tragedy, but not anonymously. On Saturday, 11 August 1979, a flotilla of three hundred and three yachts had set out in bright sunshine from the Isle of Wight but were caught in a force-ten storm as the leading boats were rounding the Fastnet Lighthouse. It was the worst race tragedy of recent times. Tom was working in NET at the time and did not cover it, but, a sailor himself, he was deeply shocked. And there is a horrible symmetry between that disaster and the eighteen deaths he did cover less than a week after his return to RTÉ. (His wife's prophecy, that he would hate PR, had come to pass: he had stuck it out for just over a year and a half.)

Cork Local Radio, later axed in an RTÉ rationalisation move, was still on the air at the time. It shared an office on Union Quay in the city with the national station and, as is common with all local radio stations, was an outlet for local complaints.

On the morning of Friday, 1 August 1980, the reception desk at the station fielded a couple of angry calls to be passed on to whoever was on air at the time. The callers were fuming about CIE. Yet again, they said,

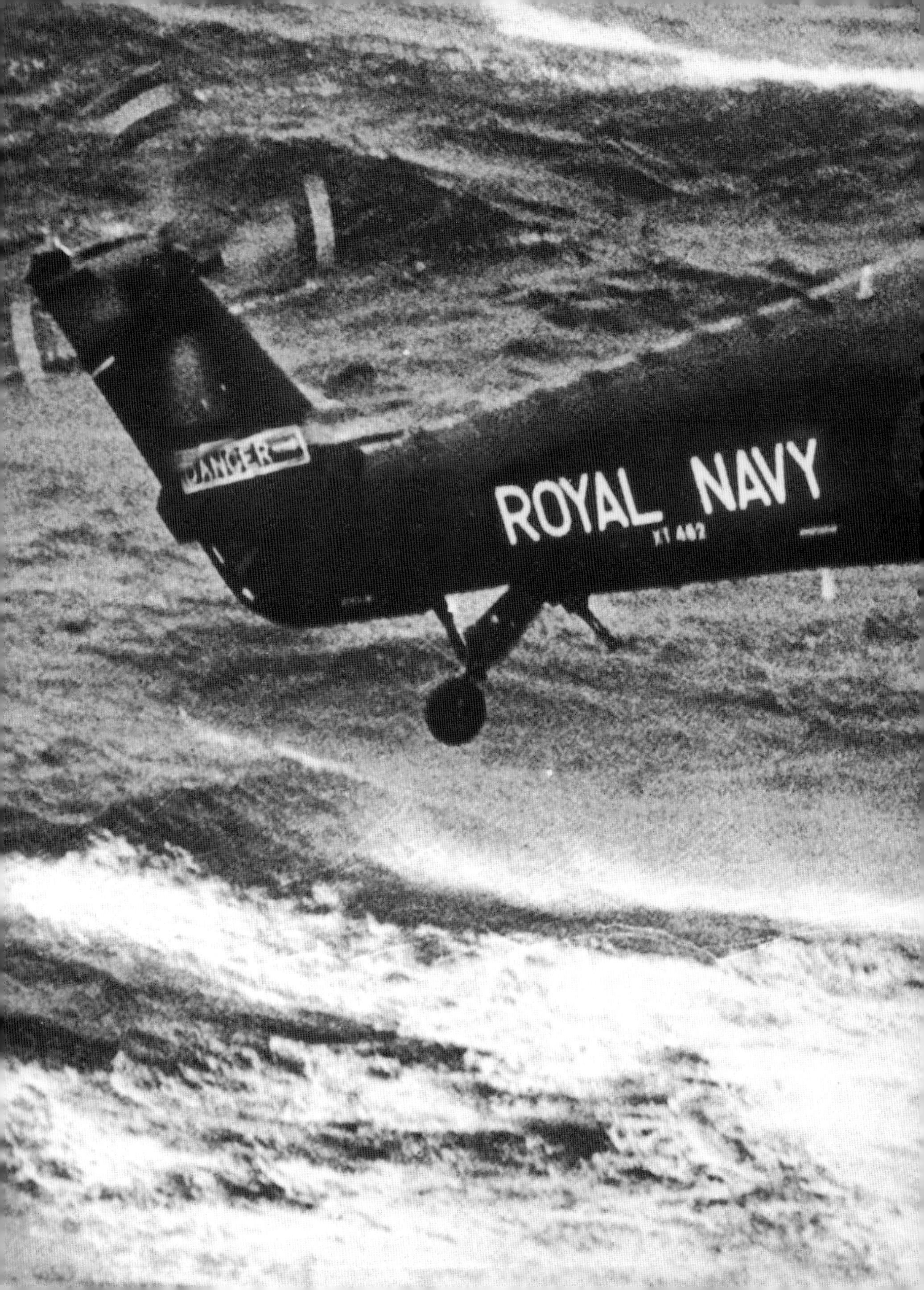
DANGER
ROYAL NAVY

the express train from Dublin was late – leaving them hanging about.

'I checked with the railway and – typical CIE – it was "Yeah, train delayed."'

A few minutes later there was a further call from the station concourse to him directly: 'They're telling us nothing. All they'll say is that "The train is delayed."'

This time, something about the tone pinged on McSweeney's experienced antennae. He rang one of his own railway contacts and, unusually, could get no information whatsoever. 'I was being passed from A to B.'

Then another call came in: this was a person in the fire service, who told him that the major emergency disaster plan for Cork had been called into action. 'And I said to myself, "Christ! It's to do with the railway."'

He immediately jumped into his car and drove to Glanmire railway station (now Kent), 'and there were people all over the place, waiting for relatives and so on. This was the Friday leading into the August bank holiday weekend and the train from Dublin was expected to be packed.'

On his way into the station, McSweeney, a well-known figure in Cork, was accosted by several people: 'There's something terribly wrong, Tom, they're giving us no explanation – they're holding something back from us. What's going on?'

He went to the station master's office: 'We can't tell you anything. You have to get on to Head Office."

'Now, when you're told to get on to Head Office, you know there's something seriously wrong.'

He rushed back to his own office and 'dashed off a line to Dublin – would they check if there was anything wrong'. He didn't have to wait for a response because a call came in to say, 'There's big trouble in Buttevant.'

He rounded up cameraman Roy Hammond and soundman Brian O'Mahoney, and the three of them – with the former in his own van – tore up the road towards Buttevant. They came to an abrupt halt at a huge traffic jam just outside Mallow. 'Lines and lines of cars.'

Next thing, an ambulance screamed past them 'so I pulled out behind it and waved at Roy to follow me'.

But the Gardaí stopped them as they got close to Buttevant railway station. 'They wouldn't let us go any further. "You can't get in here. No press! No press!"'

Tom argued, but the law was adamant so they turned around and stopped a little way down the road to have a hurried conference. 'Look,' said the reporter, 'we'll drive back down the road, find a side road and we'll follow the railway line until we come to a bridge . . .'

So they did that. When they came to the first railway bridge, they got out of their vehicles and, hefting their weighty equipment, climbed up the side of the cutting and slid down the embankment on to the railway line. 'Then we could see it. I see it to this day in my mind. Every time I hear the name "Buttevant" or go through Buttevant I can see it.

'We started to run along the railway line and – I can still see it – there was the engine and the first carriages in the siding, and the rest of the train was at the platform with the carriages off the line. That engine was clearly in the siding.'

Spotting the intrusion, CIE officials and Gardaí immediately ran towards them, waving at them to turn back, but they continued onwards, 'and I said to Roy, "Start filming! Start filming!"'

'So we had the pictures then. They were shouting at us, "You can't come in here, you can't come in here," and I was saying back, "Too late, we see it! We see it! We have the pictures! No point in stopping us!"'

'We headed onwards to the platform and the usual kind of row started, shouting at us and all that,' but Roy, who was a seasoned

hack, kept his camera rolling.

'And there it was. What clearly happened was that it had hit points.'

The three RTÉ men continued to protest that, since they already had the story and the pictures to prove it, they should be allowed to stay to report the accident. 'There were ambulances and medics around the carriages, and we knew there had to be people dead, but we didn't know how many.'

Their demands to stay were denied. 'We were ignominiously thrown out.'

Tom went into full reporter mode. He alerted his head office in Dublin about what had happened, then rang his own office at Union Quay: 'Get an OB [Outside Broadcast] unit up here. As fast as you can. We should be broadcasting from here.'

Seeing this activity, 'someone from CIE realised that this couldn't be covered up', and finally agreed to let them into a side office from which, as soon as the OB unit arrived and set up, McSweeney and his colleagues began to record.

Tom himself went out on the tracks to interview a CIE official. 'He stood there, denying to me that the train had come off the points.

But I could see it – "It's there, look – there's the points. I can see what happened."'

'There is nothing wrong technically. We have to investigate. It's too early. We cannot say—'

'But I can see it! It's there! Look where I'm pointing!'

'It's too early to say. We cannot say what caused this accident. We have to have an investigation.'

'I can see what caused it!'

'We cannot say what caused this accident.'

And so on.

Two tracks ran through Buttevant railway station, the up line to Dublin and the down line towards Cork. That day, within the ambit of the station, there had been movements, of ballast cleaners and so forth, from one line to the other across the points in question. These, installed four months previously and therefore relatively new, had not yet been connected to a signal box and were still being operated manually.

The main conclusion of the inquiry that was held later in Mallow was that the accident occurred because 'a set of unconnected facing points on the down main line at Buttevant station were partly or wholly made into the down siding when the 10.00 ex Dublin passenger train reached them and the train, which was travelling at about 65 m.p.h., was diverted into the siding and derailed'.

'Diverted into the siding and derailed'. Clipped language for what can happen when more than four hundred tons of metal, wood, human beings and baggage slam to a halt against an obstruction.

An engineer, Seán Heneghan, testified to the inquiry that:

The speed recorder from the locomotive of the derailed train was recovered intact and it indicated speeds between 68 and 70 m.p.h. as the train approached the Down Home signal. These speeds were maintained until the locomotive had gone about

33 yards beyond the nose of the Down line facing points where the speed dropped to 65 m.p.h. over a distance of about 65 yards when rapid deceleration commenced and the speed dropped to zero over a further 35 yards.

A motorist, Gabriel O'Callaghan, was stopped at the closed level crossing just beyond Buttevant station. He testified 'that just before the Down passenger train passed over the crossing, he heard an engine hooting more than he felt was normal. At about the same time someone on the Signal Cabin veranda was shouting. After the train passed he saw a cloud of dust in the station.'

Unaware of the approaching express train, a railway man had been working on those points with a bar, trying to lever out a wooden wedge (a 'scotch') that had changed their direction into the siding. He estimated for the inquiry that it usually took between five and six minutes to change the direction of the points and secure them: 'There was a total of eight sets of keys and he used different-sized safety pins to identify keys for locks on the down line from keys for locks on the up line.' The worker was not wearing a watch and, according to his evidence to the inquiry later, 'was unaware of the Regulation dealing with the securing of unconnected points that had been published in the Weekly Circular in 1977'.

While still working with his bar, he heard shouting and, again, according to the Inquiry report: '. . . he looked up and saw the passenger train approaching only about 300 yards away. Despite making a desperate attempt to re-make the points for the main line he could not shove them over before jumping clear as the train reached them . . .'

Hanna Sheahan, a member of the Red Cross for decades, was making lunch at home. Her phone rang. The caller asked her to contact her son-in-law, who was in the construction business since he needed to borrow a crane. The caller explained why.

Hanna made a fast series of phone calls, summoning other Red Cross volunteers. They worked until midnight, extracting passengers from under the wrecked wooden-framed carriages, covering the dead with yellow plastic sheets and stretchering them to the makeshift morgue CIE had set up in a waiting area at the station, transporting the injured to hospitals.

A helicopter joined in the rescue effort. To Tom McSweeney, all of these rescuers were heroic, 'ambulance people, doctors, nurses, the helicopter crew . . .' It took place in full view of the press because, having thrown up its hands, CIE now allowed unfettered access to the scene. And until the day he dies McSweeney will be haunted by what he saw inside those carriages.

I have no wish here to trigger more pain for the victims injured that day, or the relatives bereaved, so I won't detail what he saw – the blood, the severed limbs, arms caught around seats. On going into the

Eighteen people died that Friday.

temporary morgue, he found it 'respectful and quiet'. People from the town had brought in blankets to cover the bodies, but Buttevant's was a small country station and this waiting area was 'old, and dusty and a bit rundown'.

The incongruity struck him with force. 'These were people who were expecting to be in Cork within an hour, probably talking to each other. People on their bank-holiday outing, trusting in the system. And now dead. Laid out.'

It was coming up to the *Nine O'Clock News* on television and he had to treat this awful event as a professional. Knowing that RTÉ was continuing to report that nine people had been killed in the crash, he counted the bodies. He asked a technician independently to confirm his count. Their counts tallied at eighteen.

He telephoned the newsroom with the update – and ran into another system. RTÉ would not broadcast the figure unless CIE confirmed it. The count remained at nine.

McSweeney, outraged, threatened to resign: 'They wouldn't take my word for it! I was furious. Absolutely furious.' It is a sideshow to the story, but when people cannot find focus for their own grief and horror they tend to fasten on proxies.

He still suffers from flashbacks, the images of those mangled bodies now mingled with those vaporising on the decks of the Betelgeuse. And he is haunted by speculation: 'What must that man have thought when he saw the express train coming at him and he couldn't get the points back?'

He never talks about the 'grisliness' of what he saw that day in *Buttevant* or what he imagines happened in Bantry, and this interview has stirred up a lot of silt. 'I hear nowadays of everybody getting counselling for this, that and the other thing. Nobody ever gave us counselling. 'Maybe I do talk, a bit, to Kathleen – but why is it that life is cut so quickly from people just going about their business? And nobody was accountable?'

Nowadays he has no respect at all – none – for establishment systems. 'The disregard of people to own up to what's wrong and accept the responsibility. Bloody CIE fella trying to deny what I could see in front of my eyes.' His voice rises with the effort he makes to repress his fury: 'Telling you in front of your eyes that you're not seeing what you're seeing? With your own eyes?

'"Who put an express train into a siding?"

'"Oh, well, there'll have to be an investigation."

'"It shouldn't be in there."

'"We can't comment on that."'

He covered the inquiry from which the quotes above have been taken and when he came back to 'normal' work afterwards, 'That attitude of CIE had changed me in everything. I became very . . .'

He can't find the word.

'I wouldn't accept the word of authority any more. I'd check everything.'

But as he sat through the lengthy inquiry proceedings in the Hibernian Hotel in Mallow, he also realised he couldn't blame any individual on the track that day. Those workers were rarely if ever tested on their knowledge of the manuals and circulars CIE regularly sent round to its frontline railway staff. As technology changed, they were rarely if ever sent on refresher courses.

As for the accident itself, about the nightmares of the people affected: 'I think with country people they kind of put it in a box.' And, in his view, in that inquiry room, there certainly was never any air of 'We killed eighteen people'.

'"It was the points that killed them."'

Grace Under Fire

Kidnapped! Dr Tiede Herrema

It was his own calm courage that saved Tiede Herrema from being killed. The Dutchman, who ran Ferenka, a large industrial unit outside Limerick, was kidnapped just two hundred yards from his home in Castletroy when he was on his way to work on 3 October 1975 and bundled into a 'safe-house' near Mountmellick in Co. Laois.

1410 St Evin's Park, Monasterevin, October 1975. Kidnap hostage, the Dutch industrialist Dr Tiede Herrema, remains captive.

The demand of his IRA kidnappers, Marion Coyle, who was nineteen, and Eddie Gallagher, twenty, was for the release of three Republican prisoners, Kevin Mallon, Jim Hyland and the English-woman Rose Dugdale, with whom Gallagher had a relationship.

Within days, the kidnappers had moved their victim from Laois to an upstairs bedroom of a council house at 1410 St Evin's Park in Monasterevin. Gardaí, who had mounted a massive countrywide search, learned this and mounted an early-morning raid but withdrew.

Captured: Kidnapper Marion Coyle.

The kidnappers were armed.

A long, drawn-out siege ensued, attracting journalists and film crews from all over the world. Throughout, Dr Herrema displayed extraordinary courage in that, although he was blindfolded, closely confined, verbally abused and threatened with a loaded gun, he never panicked or gave up but, having soon established that Marion Coyle was by far the more callous of his two gaolers, worked steadily and calmly to forge a relationship with Eddie Gallagher. He told Gay Byrne during a long interview that 'she would have shot him. He had no doubt whatsoever about that. He knew that she was the tough one. She wanted him dead and he felt she was on the verge of it several times. He wasn't afraid of him [Gallagher] – he was just a little fella.'

The two kidnappers gave themselves up on 7 November, but not before Gallagher had presented his victim with a souvenir: the bullet from the gun that had been held to his head. Yet the Dutchman is on record as disagreeing with the length of the sentences the pair received: twenty-five years for Gallagher, twenty for Coyle. "That was too long. They were only children. Just imagine a young man of twenty going to gaol for twenty-five years. That is terrible. I see them as children with a lot of problems. If they were my children, I'd do my utmost to help them."

After Dr Herrema's release, and his return to live in Holland with his wife, Elizabeth, the Ferenka factory was closed with the loss of hundreds of jobs. He has donated his cache of personal papers to the University of Limerick. The souvenir bullet was not included.

There were so many journalists in Monasterevin during the siege, for so long with very little to do, that the anecdotes are legion, not least because of the sangfroid of the Garda charged with briefing them on what was happening. Superintendent Tom Kelly had perfected the art of waffle: he made lengthy statements and answered every question with seeming thoroughness while giving away absolutely no

With his wife Elizabeth, Dr Herrema shows the bullet from the gun held to his head.

Captured: Kidnapper Eddie Gallagher.

information.

Garda ombudsman Conor Brady, ex-editor of the *Irish Times*, was but a humble reporter on the scene and on the occasion of the thirtieth anniversary of the siege, writing in the late, lamented *Village Magazine*, he reports the following exchanges, which give a flavour of the superintendent's poker-faced attitude.

Reporter: 'Is it true, Superintendent, that the kidnappers asked for sandwiches and that the Gardaí arranged for these to be sent in?'

Press officer: 'It would be correct to say that certain digestible items, normally placed between slices of bread, were requested and provided.'

Reporter: 'Superintendent, the kidnappers and Dr Herrema seem to have no access to the toilet in the house. Can you confirm that?'

Press officer: 'I'm sorry. I'm not privy to these arrangements.'

Nice one, eh? It's the way he tells 'em.

The superintendent obviously intended this pun, but there are rich pickings in this vein within the game of soccer, whose commentators supply us with a constant stream of 'Colemanballs' – coined by *Private Eye* magazine to make famous the verbal gaffes of British commentator, David Coleman such as: 'Manchester United are buzzing around the goalmouth like a lot of red bluebottles.'

His and others' soccer slips have become the subject of anorak collections. 'Poland nil, England nil, though England are now looking the better value for their nil' – Barry Davies.

'The lad got over-excited when he saw the whites of the goalpost's eyes' – Steve Coppell, Radio 5 Live.

'I'm going to make a prediction – it could go either way' – Ron Atkinson.

The genre has expanded to include memorable utterances such as this, screamed from the Norwegian commentary box after Norway beat England for probably the first time since Noah built his Ark: 'Lord Nelson! Lord Beaverbrook! Sir Winston Churchill! Sir Anthony Eden! Clement Attlee! Henry Cooper! Lady Diana! Maggie Thatcher! Can you hear me, Maggie Thatcher? Your boys took one hell of a beating. Your boys took one hell of a beating!'

And here's Eamon Dunphy, in Bill O'Herlihy's studio, after Norway beat us: 'Just think of the Irish children crying going to their beds last night!'

Bill: 'But, Eamon, what about the happy children in Norway?'

Happy Out
Billo and Italia '90

'Eamon Dunphy is much misunderstood.'

Eh? Misunderstood?

'Misunderstood' is the last adjective I would have applied to the soccer analyst, but our Bill is adamant. He is responding to a question about the TV on-air rows begun and rants vented by Dunphy against the blazer brigade, 'rubbish' players, the selectors, the establishment, other media – 'Not you, John!' (But even against Gilesy during one long-running and very public falling-out.)

The Big Kahuna, O'Herlihy himself, has not escaped the sandpaper tongue, 'Yeah, sometimes he gives me a bollocking,' but his love remains undimmed: 'I've enjoyed working with Eamon Dunphy. I find him a fascinating person – more to him than a soccer pundit and ex-player. I got to know him as a person and respect him, and he respects

The three musketeers: Giles, Dunphy and O'Herlihy, September 1998.

185

me and we work together wonderfully. He has a very good sense of humour and you can jolly him out of things. The rows I had with him over the years were easily managed and my only concern with him is around the programme. Sometimes I think I give him too much latitude, but sometimes, I think, when he's on a rant I go after him too hard.'

He refers to both Dunphy and John Giles as 'consummate broadcasters in their own styles. If I was in trouble in any programme, if I was struggling, these guys would get me out of it.' And he believes that the role of panel chairman is frequently misunderstood. 'A good chairman doesn't dominate. The function is to showcase the strength and knowledge of the people you're talking to, not your own knowledge.'

Does he know that there is a very entertaining YouTube strand called Eamon Dunphy Rants?

He is astonished: 'Is there?'

Yes, there is.

'Of course, I'm not the YouTube generation.'

No, he's not. He characterises himself, probably with accuracy, as a very conventional, conservative guy, who espouses old-fashioned values, such as courtesy, respect, love of family and his Maker.

We are meeting in the office of his public-relations company, O'Herlihy Communications. It is tucked discreetly into a Dublin laneway – so discreetly, it has to be said, that it is hard to find.

Within, the boss's quarters are just as unprepossessing. I have always associated the letters 'PR' with acres of shiny marble, walls of pristine glass and desks that could accommodate a practice game of tennis, and the effect here is modest, even homely.

His arrival into the room has been jovial, with a firm handshake and that ready smile we all know. But there is a watchfulness about him. And when his face is in repose or in listening mode, it is quite serious, if not exactly glum. I am on notice. The man knows the score and maybe there is a line we will not cross. Maybe.

The purpose of interviewing Bill, however, is not to discuss Eamon, but principally to recall the glory days of Italia '90. Remember when we were all avidly following the team and Jack Charlton? When we threw house parties to watch communally, or paid big money to see the matches on giant screens?

For a magical few years following our first ever admittance to the sixteen left standing in a major international soccer tournament – the European Cup in 1988 – we were all interested in putting the rest of the world under pressure. This is when 'Ireland' became 'The Lads' and cheering them on enabled us temporarily to forget our personal and economic woes and the septic news from Northern Ireland. This was not about football (let's annoy Dunphy!), it was a chance for us put-upon Irish to climb, blinking, out of our Celtic gloom to bask in the international sun. To indulge in safe, sanctioned and joyful patriotism.

Bill actually agrees. 'I thought that the World Cup was an outstanding example of the country coming together.' He credits RTÉ in that because, corporately, it had made a conscious decision to turn a soccer programme into an all-inclusive national event. 'We had GAA people involved and all kinds. It tapped into a terrific national mood. The mood of celebration and of people coming together was even bigger than when the Pope came to Ireland. It was a wonderful, wonderful time. We walked tall and smiled a lot and the sense of community was terrific. I remember being asked by people if I was disappointed not to be in Italy for Italia '90 and I said no. I wouldn't have missed being in Dublin under any circumstances.'

During that World Cup tournament, especially during Ireland's games, O'Herlihy's panel reflected that sense of excitement although 'it was a controversial studio in one respect because the guys I was working with, primarily Eamon and John, didn't believe that Jack Charlton was getting as much out of the team as he should. It's only now, I think, that people know how good a team that was. It was a great Irish team by any standards or level. The bottom line, though, was that the guys felt there was far more in the team, with the players we had, than Jack's style of tight discipline allowed.

On the other hand, 'You can't take anything away from Jack because he did get us to Germany, to Italy and to the US – nobody could argue about that – but the guys had the feeling that he was very happy just to get us to Italy in the first place. To get as far as the second round.'

Well, that we did. Remember Genoa?

'Genoa was an extraordinary occasion. When it came to the penalties, the whole country came to a standstill.' (For the YouTube generation, we are referring to the match with Romania, on the result of which depended the Lads' progression. It went to penalty five, the last boot.)

Even the proceedings at an important EU meeting at Dublin Castle were temporarily suspended. 'I remember, God rest both their souls, RTÉ showed a shot of Val Dorgan [a journalist for the *Cork Examiner*], one of my heroes, fantastic range of writing skills,' and John Healy [writer and guru of Ireland's west.] Then George Hamilton magnificently said: "The nation holds its breath."'

We did. All of us.

'The most extraordinary thing about that last penalty was that it was taken by Dave O'Leary, who came on as a sub for only part of the game and he had volunteered. He wasn't a young fella but he was regarded as the best centre-half in England. Not by Jack, though; Mick McCarthy was not considered in the same league at all but he suited Jack's tactics.'

Coolly, O'Leary stared at the ball. His approach to it was

The save of his life: Packie Bonner, Genoa, 25 June, 1990.

measured, his kick firm, the Romanian goalie was floored and Ireland was through to the quarter-finals.

The Irish TV cameras instantly conveyed the national exhalation in the stadium and at home, including, back at that European summit, a clear view of tears running down the face of Val Dorgan. 'He was actually crying, you could see it.'

Val was not crying alone. We were all crying. And laughing and hugging and dancing. Even in the studio, where the reaction was 'absolute jubilation. We got up and actually danced around the studio. I don't think the punters ever saw that.'

We didn't because we were too busy exhaling and crying and cheering, but what we did see on our screens, having disentangled ourselves from our neighbours' bear hugs, was the ecstatic grin on the face of our supposedly objective sports anchor. 'People sometimes describe us as killjoys because we're analysing. We are a bit detached and I suppose you could see that we don't always join in on the occasion. And I always say, "We're not fans with typewriters!"'

Bill lends a hand or two, RTÉ studio, 25 June 1990.

In this case, though, that is exactly what they were. All of them. Even Eamon, but particularly Bill. 'In this case the analysis was gone . . .' Gone as far as the donning of a comic green hat, out of which protruded two huge floppy hands. This hat had belonged to the son of the floor manager in the studio that day 'and I took it off him . . .'

For Bill O'Herlihy, that penalty was 'the greatest moment that I've ever experienced in sport on television by a long, long way. The whole Italia '90 was fantastic, but specifically that penalty shoot-out.'

He subsequently interviewed Jack Charlton about those penalties and was a little surprised by the manager's take on it. 'He gave very little praise. I was saying it was very hard to take that final penalty and he was saying it was much harder to take the first penalty – but I think that, in the circumstances, that last penalty was an extraordinary act of courage and showed unbelievable temperament.'

Since becoming a sports anchorman, O'Herlihy has 'done' all the World Cups, European Football Championships and Rugby World Cups but, studio-bound, has never actually attended any of them. (Had Ireland qualified for the 2008 European championship, he and his team had plans – and authorisation – to go. But we didn't and they didn't – 'So that's that!') He has covered every Olympic Games since Munich in 1972 – with the exception of 1984 when he was floored by a heart-attack.

He readily acknowledges that he has one of the best jobs in Ireland. Apparently, when Graham Souness joined the analysis team for the last World Cup, he was warned that he was perceived by 'an awful lot of people to be anti-Irish'. Souness, a Scot, was 'aghast. "And isn't Dickie Rock my wife's cousin?"' And although it had nothing to do with that shock, it did take the Scot a few outings to realise the difference between sitting on an RTÉ panel and its equivalent on the British stations he was used to. 'He was a bit diffident for the first two days' until the penny dropped and he realised that 'on RTÉ you can say what you want and actually call a spade a spade. You can't, he said, on the other stations. He loved it from then on.'

So does O'Herlihy. He knows, too, that on this earth, he leads one of the best lives. Happy family, ownership of his own successful company, doyen of the sports fraternity, even Sports Personality of the Year in 2007. (And he's from Cork! Talk about cups running over!) 'Yes, I'm living the dream. No argument about that.'

Sports journalism had not been his lifelong ambition: 'All I ever wanted to be was a current affairs journalist,' following in the footsteps of his grandfather, Willie O'Herlihy, who had been editor of the *Cork Examiner*, a position of some eminence in the Emirate of Cork.

He was received with open arms when, at the age of fifteen, he took his chances there. 'You have a terrific pedigree,' burbled Tom Crosbie, scion of the long-tailed family who own de paper. 'Any O'Herlihy who wants a job in the *Examiner* will have no difficulty here.'

He started, as all trainee journalists once did, in the Reading Room, unlike today's young masters of journalism who deal almost solely with digital recording, data transfer and pixels. Its walls and ceiling brown from the cigarette smoke of its occupants, the reading room of the *Examiner* was situated beside the clattering print floor and its ear-splitting Linotype machines where reporters' and advertising copy was set.

A proof of each page, rolled around the original copy for comparison, was delivered from the print floor through a chute to a posse of readers, each in a cubicle and attended by a copy holder. The reader's task was to spot mistakes and misprints while reading the page proof aloud to the copy holder. The copy holder's complementary job was to listen, checking there was nothing missing from the reporter's story, no advertisement for day-old chicks or bonhams absent from its allotted advertising space. It was where they imbibed the newspaper's house style and learned to be accurate.

O'Herlihy's mother was 'appalled' at the notion of her son abandoning his Leaving Cert, but she was powerless against the might of his ambition, and abandon it he did. Quite quickly he was promoted to work on the afternoon paper (d'*Echo*) on which, still only sixteen and a half, he became a sub-editor. 'It was a wonderful place to work.'

As a 'one-eyed man in the valley of the blind', he had done some sports reporting into Harry Thuillier's *Saturday Sports Show* on Radio Éireann, had come to the attention of various interested parties in both radio and television and, as a result, had been asked to do a TV interview with an old woman in Cappoquin hospital, a survivor of the *Lusitania* disaster.

'I had no interest in television, I didn't think I had the voice, or the appearance – and when I see myself nowadays on *Reeling Back the Years* and so on, I ask myself how, in God's name, did anyone think I had talent? But they were stuck for someone.'

It took 'ages' to get usable stuff from the bedridden survivor, but having viewed the result on the following day, Frank Hall, who was at that stage a bigwig in the station, issued an instruction that from then on young Bill O'Herlihy was to do all of RTÉ's feature work out of Cork. The *Examiner*'s management proved to be magnanimous about this arrangement, provided that their reporter's appearances were credited to the paper during transmission and that they got use of the stories.

But then he was offered a full-time job on *Seven Days*, flagship of RTÉ's television current affairs schedule.

Didn't want it. No. Like all Cork people, he didn't want to leave Cork.

Didn't want to leave Cork? 'That's all right,' said the head of TV Programmes, Muiris MacConghail. 'You can be based in Cork. Cork has an airport. I'll want you to go to China. I'll want you to go to the States. I'll want you to go to the Middle East.'

Okey-doke. Our hero signed, and on a September morning he went up to Dublin to attend the planning meetings for the coming season. Day one in the New Life.

On day two Séamus Smith, the number two in television, looked with some puzzlement at their new signing, having realised that something odd was going on: 'Are you with us or are you not with us?'

'With, of course,' said O'Herlihy, cheerily, 'but as you know I'm going to be based in Cork.'

'You're in your arse going to be based in Cork. You can't work for *Seven Days* out of Cork. I'll tell you what you do now. Pack your suitcase, kiss your mother goodbye, because you're coming up here and you're staying here.'

'But – but . . .'

There were no further buts.

The *Seven Days* assemblage was known for indefatigable independence and tough, forensic questioning of interviewees, particularly government politicians and spokespersons. And, in O'Herlihy's view, the last straw for the Fianna Fáil government of the day was a programme on the implications of a 'straight' (as opposed to proportional representation) electoral system for Ireland. The show was transmitted while a referendum on the proposal was in the air and, he believes, contributed hugely to its comprehensive defeat.

He also believes it led directly to the Money-lending Tribunal, arising from an investigation into money-lending by the Seven Days team. 'I think Fianna Fáil decided that they were going to put manners on RTÉ current affairs, and they picked on the money-lending programme as the way to do that. It was a lot to do with Muiris and with the government's attitude to RTÉ as an arm of government propaganda.'

That tribunal resulted in purgatory for RTÉ staff and executives, who appeared with other witnesses 'for fifty two and a half days before a panel of three judges'.

O'Herlihy's own appearance on the witness stand still rankles for many reasons, not least the pedantry of the way in which he was questioned. I know it is a sore subject, not only because of the anger with which he relates it but because, prior to this interview, I had heard the same passion in his voice while he recounted it on *Conversations with Dunphy* on RTÉ Radio One. 'One day, it was day three, I think, I came back after lunch and he [the judge] asked me to define the word "classic". I asked if this was in the context of the script.

'"No, no," he said, "I want a precise definition."'

The broadcaster, whose vocabulary is not sluggish, pooched around, offering various meanings and interpretations but then, with some ceremony, His Lordship opened a dictionary and intoned the precise meaning of the word: 'a supreme example of the ordinary'. Then he expressed surprise that 'a reporter of your experience on a programme of the stature of *Seven Days*' would not know its precise definition.

'I'm not exaggerating. It's included in the report.'

The Money-lending Tribunal, which was traumatic for RTÉ in

Young Turk, 1969.

many ways, has been well documented elsewhere. For here, suffice it to say that the current affairs department, whose jewel had been Seven Days, was left in tatters. There were nervy meetings, rumours and counter-rumours that the show, even the entire department, was being axed. 'It was an extraordinary time,' he says, but he is anxious to stress that throughout there was huge support from director general Tom Hardiman and those on the top floor of the station.

In this miasma, O'Herlihy was offered a transfer to the news division or to 'light' current affairs, but wanted neither. Six months later, however, when the situation had calmed somewhat and he was working away, 'one of the Authority members contacted the director general, Tom Hardiman, and said, 'O'Herlihy has done a programme in the midlands and it's not authentic . . .'

Instantly, a red warning flag flashed up. 'This word "authentic" had been used in the Tribunal report . . .'

The film was reassembled – and not only the film but the notes and research – and the programme found to be 'authentic' in every detail. 'But I knew then that if I was ever to do a very serious programme this word "authentic" would hound me at least for a period of time. You have to be realistic. So I said to myself, "If I was RTÉ I'd say that this guy, O'Herlihy, is becoming a bit of a millstone around the neck of current affairs."'

He asked for a transfer to sport.

It was granted – to the displeasure of the department head, Micheál Ó hEithir. 'The very first day I appeared it was "Well, Bill, I don't want you. You haven't got the right image for sport"' Ó hEithir also told his new recruit that he would not be allowed to broadcast 'for about six months at a minimum. It was an open-plan office so everyone knew . . .'

That was on a Thursday.

On the Friday, Ó hEithir called him in and gave him a marking to do an interview.

'I thought you said I wouldn't be on for six months.'

'That was yesterday.'

From then on he was on air all the time, despite some calls to the switchboard complaining that it was very sad to see poor Bill O'Herlihy sink so low as to be reading the racing results. They did not impinge. 'I had a job – I was just married. And to be fair to Mick O Hehir, about two months later he came out very publicly into the office and put his arm around me and said, "I know people think I didn't want you, but thanks be to Christ you're here."'

'Which was nice.'

At that time the sports department fixture list was very predictable, as was the roster for its staff. 'You knew exactly what you were doing six months down the line.' And, just as predictably, perhaps, our hero got bored. 'I felt I was just coasting along. That I wasn't doing anything of any substance . . .'

From stage left, enter Brindley Advertising, whose staff were feeling the pressure of public-relations demands on their time. 'They wanted to start up an arm of the company to deal with it. They'd fund it for two years and then I could have it.'

He had always been interested in business, took the offer and, with phones ringing and computers humming across the corridor, here we are sitting comfortably around the boardroom table of the consequent creation.

Unlike Mike Murphy, he has found that his two lives, in broadcasting and business, dovetail nicely. The business side is the more stressful: 'Sometimes I'd go into RTÉ for a big match and I'd be very stressed, and as the programme came into being, I'd be very relaxed.'

His cardiologist doesn't believe him: 'That can't be right.'

'But it is. It's only a match.'

He feels 'very lucky' to be a regular on television, particularly in the chair he occupies, and he would never rock RTÉ's boat: 'By nature I'm not a boat-rocker, I'd say of all the presenters I'd be the most placid.'

Given his history, training, PR and broadcasting perspectives, he is in a good position to comment on the present media landscape and is (diffidently) touchy about the negativity 'too often' displayed in the media about traditional morals and ethics in this country. 'They have hobby-horses about the Church and so on and that's having an effect on the values in Ireland.'

He does accept that, to an extent, he is shooting the messenger here: 'I don't deny that the media did play a valuable role in exposing child abuse and so on. And, yes, it does seem to me that the Church has disqualified itself in many instances, Bishop Casey and so forth. No one could ever accuse the media wrongly in their role in that story.'

We are teetering on a border beyond which he sees the threat of exposing his personal values – but we plunge ahead regardless. 'Look, this is where I'd be prejudiced, because I'm a churchgoing person.'

This goes right to the heart of the changes in Irish society since the time when it was understood that you'd meet all of your neighbours, their grannies and their infants at Sunday Mass, the Holy Week ceremonies, the men's and women's sodalities and the May devotions. Although he insists he is not apologising for his deeply held beliefs, he does sound defensive, as if making an admission. Remember, this is a confident public figure in his seventh decade. He has seen and done it all and has little left to prove, few to impress. His hesitancy, therefore, is a revealing insight into how Irish society has changed and how pluralism is anything but. 'There's a sense now that nobody goes to church: I try to go to Mass every morning. That's so out of line with current thinking.'

We have crossed the border. 'My experience is that if you're not in line with the agenda of the day, you're going to get screwed. The general media fail to recognise that there's a very substantial mass of people who are believers and who really aren't represented. I think that people like me who go to church are being perceived in the current climate as cranks. Which isn't true, and I think we've lost an awful lot. There's a lack of balance. Attackers get the airtime and one of the things I like immensely about the new Archbishop of Dublin, Diarmuid Martin, is that he sticks up for what he wants. In the club, follow the rules. That's what it should be.'

Not surprisingly, O'Herlihy sprang from a very traditional family, rosary every night. 'It was ingrained in us, not forced.'

Have his two brushes with death – his heart-attack in 1984 and more recent fight with cancer – deepened his faith?

He's careful: 'I made sure that if I was to shuffle off this mortal coil, I was OK to meet my Maker.' Then he goes for it: 'Look, my father had a fantastic belief in Our Lady and I have that as well. He also believed that the Lord would stay close to us. And I don't see any point in not trusting. If things are to happen they're to happen.'

That's almost Buddhist?

'Well, if it is then I'm a Buddhist Catholic! At the end of the day, I put myself in the hands of the Lord.'

He realises he has walked us onto terrain that is even more difficult than a statement of simple religious practice. 'I've never discussed this. I would be the worst possible person to be involved in a theological argument.'

His faith is unquestioning. For instance, with populations rising towards trillions on this planet, never mind how many beings are out there within other universes, has he ever wondered how God can be personally interested in each one? How Our Lady can pick out an individual's prayer for advocacy in the midst of such Babel?

'That's what faith means. Faith means you have to accept the incomprehensible. What your mind tells you is nonsense versus what your beliefs tell you is the case. So much has been discovered that we didn't know in the past and so much remains to be discovered.'

In his view, the battle is soul versus brain, and the effort made to understand the soul's infinite truths with the puny, finite brain causes 'confusion, conflict and dissatisfaction'. For his own well-being, he prefers not to worry about what he can never understand, 'I believe implicitly that we are created by the Lord and the Lord looks after us. That doesn't mean we're dictated to, we can do what we want to do, but there is an overriding presence. Which I believe is God.'

How does he see God?

'I suppose all I see are the visuals I see in the church.' He's a little taken aback and is working it out as he speaks. 'I don't see a man with a grey beard. A lot of my beliefs are to do with Our Lady – it's a kind of father/daughter relationship. I look at Our Lady as an advocate and if I'm struggling or looking for something that is troubling me in terms of the family or anything else, I always call on Our Lady. I talk to her the way I'd talk to my mother. So the image I have is a family image: a paternalistic God and an advocate mother.'

He retreats. 'I find these things embarrassing. I feel myself to be very conventional and Catholic, very much the result of my upbringing. Very much embarrassed that I would not be able to stand up and proclaim with theological certainty what I believe in.'

It is ironic, he thinks, that his long and happy marriage to his wife, Hillary, is what used to be quaintly termed 'mixed'. 'She had a wonderful father, but he was a Freemason. I wanted an ecumenical service but I couldn't find anyone to do it.' This was, he believes, because of the strength of the *Ne Temere* decree in Ireland at the time; to defy it might have affected the careers of the clerics he approached. Eventually, he and Hillary got married in the chapel at Dublin airport.

Posterity? How will his epitaph encapsulate this straight and happy life of his?

'That's a very profound question. I have been extraordinarily lucky. I never in my life anticipated the unbelievable blessings I have received through my children and my wife. I have job satisfaction and reasonable wealth, but I put the value of my life in my family, something I have attempted to pass on. There's no greater gift a person can have.'

He claims not to think too deeply about his most precious beliefs and would clearly prefer not to. 'If I thought about these things it would destabilise me. I just believe that there is a Superior Being – and that Being is interested in me. And that Our Lady has looked after me especially during certain periods of my life.' For instance, was it coincidence that he had his heart-attack when he was in a meeting with Parc, the company who ran a hospital in Baghdad? That the meeting was in the College of Surgeons? And that one of the people there with him when he collapsed was Parc's director of medicine? As for the outcome of his more recent spat with colon cancer, it was found during surgery that it had not spread at all. 'I didn't have to have chemo or anything.' Given circumstances such as these, it is not hard to accept the gorgeous image, offered shyly, that he was, and is, living 'under Our Lady's cloak'.

I know he will worry about having revealed too much. But in this day of sour-puss cynicism, soundbites of outrage, pronouncements of secular gurus and touch-feely new-ageism, it has been terrifically refreshing to meet a glad, tradition-grounded person, even though we have strayed very far from football.

So to bring us back to Italia '90 and that shoot-out, here is my own fondest memory of that apogee of the Charlton era. It is not of the event itself.

I was driving through O'Connell Street at around six o'clock the following morning. I can't remember why, exactly – I was with the *Sunday Tribune* at the time and may have been on a deadline. The lights on the north side of the bridge were red, and as I cruised to a halt beside one of the angels guarding Daniel O'Connell, I wound down the window to enjoy the freshness of the newly washed street and the unusual sense of quiet at that normally tumultuous junction. Then, through the ticking of the engine, I heard a crooning – a sort of happy murmur.

The source proved to be a middle-aged man who, for his own entertainment, was humming a quiet '*Olé! Olé!*' while weaving his way across the plaza in front of the monument. He was carrying a limp tricolour and wearing a green jersey that bore every sign of a prolonged liquid celebration.

As he came close, he noticed my amused gaze through the car

window and stopped, swaying, while a broad and bleary grin split his face. He raised his flag and waved it at me, a gesture arrested by a loud hiccup that took him by surprise. 'Pardon!' he said, blinking, then stumbled against the statue's plinth and, flailing for support, dropped his flag.

The lights changed, but as I drove off, I watched in my wing mirror while he retrieved the tricolour, righted himself and, with the flag drooping from one hand, turned in the direction of my retreating car and raised both his arms as though addressing a victor's homecoming rally.

That for me defines Italia '90. That man was happy out, as they used to say in my Mayo schooldays. I knew exactly how he felt. Incredibly, amazingly, deliriously, the lads had kicked us through to the quarter-finals!

Nothing was impossible now, we thought, communally happy out as we surged *ad astra*. And beyond.

Welcome home!
Fans on O'Connell
Street after Genoa,
1 July, 1990.

As I'm still in the territory, I can't resist telling you a footy story about the late Raymond Smith, who worked for the Irish Independent. *Smith was one of those old-style reporters who, while regarding his profession as serious business, was a very funny raconteur when regaling the world at large about his exploits 'in the field'. These stories, usually against himself, were told in such savoury and rapid Limerick English and with such relish you could taste it in your own mouth.*

Here he is, talking to footballer Michel Platini:

Smith: 'Michel, after playing Manchester United tonight, do you feel they will soon reach the promised land by ending their long wait for the first-division title?'

(Silence.)

Smith: 'Michel, do you speak English?'

Platini: 'Yes. Do you?'

And before we leave Bill O'Herlihy's TV studio we should get a few words from Billo himself on where the glory days started. That was Stuttgart 1988 when our European Championship foray – and particularly that goal – was made all the more satisfying by the attitude of our opponents from across the Irish Sea. 'The English were very patronising in advance: they were saying how wonderful it was that Ireland had qualified for a major tournament for the first time.

'And suddenly Ray Houghton scored and we won it . . .'

Says it all, really, but not fully. We beat England, Bill, but not without engendering the type of stress against which your cardiologist warns you. The problem was Ray's timing. That ball hit the England mesh at only the sixth minute of ninety. It created euphoria for sure but left us an eighty-four-minute legacy of fluttery pulses and white-hot rosary beads. The nation couldn't hold its breath that time, Bill. Not for eighty-four bloody minutes.

We had nearly qualified for the last sixteen a few times before, but nearly never wins the race – and even this time, let's be honest, before packing our bags, we had been gloomily clutching at mathematical straws. Then, courtesy of Scotland's win over Bulgaria during the qualifiers, the maths turned out for our side, we scraped in and Jack's Army booted up for the march.

And wasn't it serendipitous that it was a Scot who shot that ball past the English goalie?

GOOOOOOAALLLLLLL!!!!!!

Come Out to Play, Ray Houghton!

Ray Houghton and I are to meet in the lobby of the Shelbourne Hotel. *Six minutes in.* As I've no doubt already demonstrated, I wouldn't know a vast amount about soccer, but I had been in Stuttgart that day on behalf of the *Sunday Tribune*, had actually been in the stadium for that historic goal, had travelled with the fans to Gelsenkirchen and so on. And, to be honest, I had been almost more impressed with the supporters than with the team. It was Jack's Army's first outing to a major tournament, so individually – and by osmosis collectively – it was clear they were determined to gain an international reputation as 'good' supporters. In an era when littering Ireland was the national hobby, it was amazing to watch these (mostly) men as they meticulously tidied away their empty beer cans and sandwich wrappers. How they led by example and tut-tutted at the laggards among them. How, on leaving each railway carriage, they did final visual checks to make sure they had not

Jack Charlton takes his lads (and lassies) to Germany, 1988.

forgotten the teeniest spill or crumb.

I wait for Houghton, searching the face (and physique) of each man who pushes through the Shelbourne's swinging doors; I am trawling furiously through my memory banks in an effort to remember what he looks like. The nearest I had come to him before was when I was standing with the thousands and thousands of people in College Green in front of the dais laden with officialdom to welcome him and his teammates home.

(By the way, one of the Dublin 'gospel facts' I have heard on numerous occasions is that Nelson Mandela was the warm-up man that day, being honoured with the freedom of Dublin and was introduced to the crowd from the podium. And that when he appeared, the crowd began to chant, 'Ooh-ah! Paul McGrath's da!' Lovely story – but Mandela received the Freedom of Dublin months later, in September of that year.)

In the Shelbourne's lobby, I notice a smallish man – not much taller than I – standing quietly beside me. Well groomed, wearing a natty business outfit and checking his mobile phone, his demeanour is unassuming.

Couldn't be him. Nah! Banker? Businessman?

I return my attention to the door.

Yet out of the corner of my eye I can see that this guy is dividing his own gaze between the swinging door and his mobile as though watching for a message.

I risk it: 'Excuse me – are you, Ray?'

'Deirdre?'

We've met.

We settle into what used to be the public tearoom of the Shelbourne Hotel and is now reserved (very strictly) for residents. Luckily, Ray Houghton is registered here – earlier that evening he had been commentating for RTÉ Sports, a new career for him.

The tea room, with its clubby, plush feel and swaggy curtains is not full and we easily find a two-seater table against the wall. Our entry has been quiet but, even so, he has been spotted by an Irish group sitting beside one of the bay windows and there's a bit of excited nudging going on. If he has seen it, he doesn't betray it. His mien is affable and obliging, he makes no pre-conditions, and accepts that the tape-recorder can roll right away.

Before we deal with Stuttgart, because Bill O'Herlihy has dealt with that penalty shoot-out against Romania in Italia '90 from a pundit's point of view, it might be good to get the perspective of someone who took part in it.

No problem. He's happy to talk about that day in Genoa where he himself successfully took one of the penalties, but 'I was trying to organise it, to be honest with you. We didn't have five. We were struggling, we only had three or four willing. More importantly, I was trying to convince Tony Cascarino to take one because he was our striker. And strikers are supposed to take penalties and he was "Nah, I don't really want one."

'You understand people when they say that. Beforehand they'll say, "Yeah, I'll take one," but when it comes to the crunch, you really have to think, Yeah, I can do this. You don't want to let your mates down, you've come a long way. Tony was worried about letting down the squad he was part of, and the fans who'd come a long way and paid a lot of money. There's a lot of responsibility and it's not only responsibility. It's doubting your own courage. 'I'd never taken a penalty professionally in my life. And I just felt confident in myself that, yeah, I could take one now. And I was trying to convince him that he should feel the same and finally I got him into my way of thinking.'

Grand. So now tell us about Dave.

'Yeah, Dave. That was another shock. You're looking around and you're saying, "Right, who's going to take one?" And Dave says, "I'll take one," and everyone's going, "Wha'?"

"Yeah," he says, "I'll take one!"'

It was that casual?

'If you'd asked me who'll not take a penalty I'd have picked Dave. It's not in his character. He was a substitute that day, he'd not long come on, and for him to put his hand up showed tremendous courage. And then he says, "I'll go fifth."

'Now if you're out of it, and you're fifth, it makes no difference because you don't have to take the penalty. But if you're the one who could make the difference, then the pressure's on you. And in fairness he took one and it was an absolutely fantastic penalty.'

There cannot be a person in Ireland at this stage who has not seen an archive TV clip of that penalty, followed immediately by the back view of Mick Byrne's ballooning shirt as, surrounded by a swarm of other green shirts, jerseys and tracksuits, they all run to envelop O'Leary and Packie Bonner who, a few minutes earlier, had made a spectacular save.

'What that did show was how tight it was. Everybody piled in. There wasn't one person who didn't run into it, it was en masse. For Ireland to qualify for the World Cup and make the quarter-final was a fantastic achievement. We'd had the Euros, that was great, but this was the World Cup. This was the world!'

Back now to the outset of that Charlton March two years earlier. Stuttgart, that iconic goal and the wild, overjoyed mood that followed. The Irish fans couldn't bear to leave the stadium after 'their' victory, but stayed in the stands, singing their hearts out for an hour after the end of the match.

'Yeah, I remember it,' he says politely, in answer to the question he has had to respond to thousands of times from that day to this wherever he has encountered an Irish person. Even the novelist Marian Keyes has written in her online newsletter how she and a party of fans, in Cyprus to attend a qualifier for the 2008 Euro, spotted a besuited Houghton quietly leaving a restaurant. The males in the party apparently spent the rest of the evening trying to contact him, even going from room to room banging on doors with a forlorn bleating of 'Ra-ay! Ra-ay!' to talk about the goal. This, remember, was twenty years after it had been scored.

I actually missed a crucial couple of seconds of the action because my view had been obscured by a curly green wig in front of my face.

But, courtesy of a grainy TV clip, it starts with a long kick from Kevin Moran, intercepted by a bunch of English defenders. In the mill that follows, John Aldridge gets his head to it, sends it across the goal mouth towards Houghton, who catapults his five feet seven and a half inches well above what seems natural. Then, seeming to feint a little to wrong-foot the England goalkeeper, Peter Shilton, he heads the ball to sail over a couple of England defenders and Shilton, before it blips neatly into the upper left-hand corner of the net.

Back to Stuttgart proper on the day where, all around me in the crowd, there was a split second of what I can only describe as stundom, even from Curly Wee Wig. There then followed an explosion of delight, the likes of which I have never encountered before or since.

The timing was good because, coincidentally, Dublin was celebrating its Millennium with the slogan 'Dublin's Great in '88', Ireland Inc was getting itself on the map and, after years of negativity and glumness, the national mood and confidence in 'our own' was growing. Some writers opine that Euro '88 – and that goal in particular – was what kick-started the party.

As for the team's homecoming from Germany and the welcome it got, does Houghton remember hanging out over the upper deck of an open-topped bus in O'Connell Street to sing, at the top of his voice, 'Who put the ball in the England net?' Then, pointing with triumphant emphasis to his chest: 'I did! I did!'

He does, rather ruefully. 'That was my brother's fault, I blame him for that. After that match in Stuttgart we went back to the hotel and Jack allowed us to see family and friends. My brother started singing, "Who put the ball in the England net? He did! He did!" So he started it.'

They had gone to Germany full of determination and vim. 'We didn't want to embarrass ourselves, we wanted to do well. England were a tough side and then we were playing Russia, who were a massive side [in that case, even though the result was a draw, in Houghton's opinion 'we played them off the pitch!'] and then we had Holland. We couldn't have got three bigger games, really, and if we had had a poor start it would have been compounded for the next game and the next. So we knew we were under pressure to do something.'

They did that. 'It's always sweet for Celts to beat England' but what made it doubly sweet was that it was the first time Ray Houghton had scored for Ireland. 'I'd gone twenty games without a goal.'

The rest of the match 'is a bit of a haze. I remember defensively we were under pressure, Packie'd made saves [in many of the match reports, Packie Bonner is said repeatedly to have had 'the game of his life'], we'd hit the woodwork. But my final memory, which is quite strange when you beat England, is of seeing Mick Byrne, the physio, blessing himself in front of the Irish fans in the stand. He's over there and he's blessing himself – look what I've done! You'd think he'd won the game!

'And Kevin Moran. It was that hot a day, and he had all this white stuff around his mouth – so dry he couldn't lick his lips. And we'd just beaten England and I'm laughing at him and there's a picture of him and me with our arms around each other, absolutely hilarious.'

Despite the on-field joy, and the certainty 'that we'd done something good', it took a while for the significance to sink into the minds of the players, perhaps because, despite the response of the fans in the stadium, they had only second-hand knowledge of the national fiesta and euphoria back in Ireland, from the RTÉ crew who were sleeping in the same hotel and who would show them some of the footage of the reaction. Remember, a large number of them had not been born in

*Houghton and
Kevin Moran.*

Ireland but were removed by maybe two generations. And the
manager was English, a fact that, in itself, had prompted bitchy media
comment about him – that, having watched Houghton's goal, he had
removed his cap and rubbed his head because he was experiencing
mixed feelings.

Houghton puts that canard to bed. 'Nothing could be further from
the truth. He was upset that people thought he'd taken his cap off
because we'd scored against England. He was sitting on the bench,
and when the goal was scored, instead of jumping forward, he jumped
straight up, and there was this massive part of the dugout over him
and he smashed his head.'

Further proof, if proof is needed, of where Jack's loyalty lay was that after the match he pulled Ray Houghton aside. 'As much as he was delighted I'd scored, he said to me, "Don't you ever score that early in a game again. I had eighty-four minutes of hell. I don't think my heart could take that again."' (His player disobeyed orders again in the USA, when Ireland was playing Italy in the Giants Stadium during the World Cup tournament in 1994. Another game he won for us.)

It was only when they saw for themselves how the pack of travelling fans was swelling – and celebrating – that they realised how big this European adventure truly was for Ireland. 'We were going to Hanover for the second game and all of a sudden there were thousands of Irish fans and we were wondering, "What's going on here?"

'And then we got to Gelsenkirchen for the match against Holland . . . I just don't know where they came from for that match. Of course, it's just across the border with Germany.'

His overall take on the European Championship is that just eight minutes before the end of the third match, against Holland, this team, on its first outing to a major competition, was still on course to get into the next round. That was no small achievement and the flight back to Dublin was riotously celebratory. 'We'd a great time.'

It was almost a relief to let loose. 'What people don't know is that for the players it's boring. The actual games, yeah, they're brilliant,

Killing time with David O'Leary, Malta, 30 May 1990

but the other side of it is sitting around, waiting. In those days we had no CDs or DVD players so we played cards . . . I played some cards, but a lot of the players played poker, which wasn't my cup of tea, and I spent a lot of time just walking around the hotel, trying to fill hours.'

Football practice, maybe?

'Yes, there's training. But how long can

you train? You can't train for five hours, much as you'd love to. And after training you're meant to go back to your room and put your feet up, but you put your feet up and what you have, in Italy, for instance, is Italian TV, and you don't understand a word of it, and there are only so many books you can read, so you're just sitting around whiling away the hours.'

That was a long time ago, of course. No such entertainment lacunae for today's pampered pitch pets.

Yet at a time when huge resources have been poured into professional football, to Houghton 'It's a surprise that in Ireland, as well as England, Scotland and Wales, they aren't producing more players. I think it's astonishing.'

To him there is no greater job in the world than to be a professional soccer player. 'You're not travelling around driving a truck for forty-five or fifty hours a week, sitting up there at the controls staring through the window at fifty-five or sixty miles an hour. You get a fantastic amount of money for not an awful lot of work. You've got fresh air, you've got the best of hotels, you've got the best of travel, you've got the holidays that hardly anyone else can compete with.'

And you're fit to enjoy it all because of all the physical training, and 'if you get the smallest of twinges or injuries, you get the best of instant medical attention'.

But surely the game itself is getting better now, given the nutrition, the training, the treatments? The motivational prospect of glittering salaries and transfer fees?

He becomes careful. 'I'm going to sound like a cynical old man when I say "not". Everyone in the Premier League, apart from the top four plus Everton, Aston Villa and Tottenham Hotspur, is playing what I call "Fear Football". They play defensively through fear of being relegated. That's the biggest harm. There's so much money lost in getting relegated, people are not playing exciting football, attractive football, free-flowing football – whatever you want to call it. Certainly not playing to entertain the fans. It's all about getting numbers behind the ball, being hard to beat.

'I look back at my time at Oxford – that was never our way of playing. You went out and played football no matter who you were playing against.'

All of that being said, he understands the desire to get those vital three points at the cost of failing to produce on-field thrills. Relegation is a big deal and not only for the players. 'A lot of people lose their jobs due to relegation.'

Like many players of the past, Houghton honed his footballing skills on the tough streets of his neighbourhood, the working-class area of Castlemilk in Glasgow ('no milk, no castles') where he was born in January 1962. 'Football's been in my blood since I can remember, since my nan bought me my first pair of Georgie Best football boots for Christmas. I was the richest boy in town. Not many others I knew had Georgie Best football boots. I learned with my mates to survive bumping into people, to get up and carry on. I practised every day. Against the wall, heading, kicking, every moment I could. How're they going to learn now?

Opposite: 19 goals for West Ham, 21 (including this one) for Fulham, November 1982.

'Now everything's controlled. If you're a good player you go to an academy when you're eight, nine, you're put into an environment where you're happy, with your mates, and you're put in with all these other specialists. Everyone thinks they're going to go on.

'The point is, how are they going to learn to take knocks, and failure, and defeat? How are they going to take being sent home when some manager decides, and they're still in their teens, that they won't make it?'

He sidetracks wistfully: 'You never let your kids out now. PlayStations. Internet. I've got a daughter [Harley: he delivered her when his wife went into labour unexpectedly], she's twelve, and she

comes in and does her homework and then she says, "Can I go in on MSN and talk to my friends?"'

He tries to limit her time on MSN to just twenty minutes, 'maximum half an hour, because, love, I don't want you to spend your life that way. . .'

He doesn't get very far.

With Harley and his three sons, he has replicated his original family of three boys and a girl. 'Both my brothers were good footballers. One was at Chelsea when he was a kid, one had trials at Derby. Luck plays a part. My luck came when I was working at J&B whisky for a short time, shipping the whisky to America. Denis Philips, a friend of mine from school, got picked up by a West Ham scout, Bruce McLaren. He never saw me play, he just came up to my house and asked me if I wanted to sign up as a schoolboy player. He took me on the back of what Denis had told him. And there was my break. I did six months, then gave up work and signed a contract with West Ham.'

That was in 1979, when he was seventeen years old. The tenacity and toughness laid down on the streets of Castlemilk stood to him at that club, but even before he joined, he was no stranger to letdowns. 'I was small and had had so many rejections between fourteen and sixteen,' that he was used to being told, 'You're a good player,' before whoever had said it went on to patronise him about his stature. He'd got used to kindly exhortations to 'Continue eating your potatoes and drinking your Guinness and eating steak and you might grow to be a big strong boy.'

What hurt most, however, was his rejection from West Ham after three years there. 'I'd scored nineteen goals for the reserves. I'd been doing the business. And when you score nineteen goals, you think, Yeah! I'm going to be playing in the first team next week.'

Instead, when contract time was up, 'I was told it might be better if I moved on. It was hard.'

This was where his resilience and stubbornness came to the fore. 'There's two ways to go, you capitulate and give up and say it's not for you, or you fight back. You just think, You know what? I'm going to prove to myself they've made a mistake!'

He fought back well enough to be given a slot at Fulham for three years, 145 games and 21 goals, until Oxford United paid £147,000 for him. And two years after that, his price went up when Liverpool paid £185,000 for his services.

This was the dream come true. 'I knew I was going to move, but I didn't really know where. I was talking to Arsenal, Brian Clough wanted me at Nottingham Forest, Leeds were interested in me, and Milan.

'Roma, I've since found out, were interested in me too, but my heart was set on Liverpool. I'd watched them as a kid, I'd loved them. I'd loved the atmosphere at Anfield, so once Kenny Dalglish [a lifelong hero] showed an interest, it was fairly easy for me.'

By that time he was also on Jack Charlton's Ireland panel alongside John Aldridge, his former teammate from Oxford United and also now at Liverpool.

Why Ireland and not Scotland? First, 'because Scotland never asked me!' Also, one suspects, it had something to do with his trial for the Scotland under-eighteens with a group of other lads and how the trials manager had separated out 'the Anglos': 'You Anglos stand over there!' Houghton was included in that group because he was living in London at the time. Not clever, Manager!

Second, it might have had quite a lot to do with his dad, who was never done talking about Ireland and Buncrana, his birthplace, 'and when Jack came in, it was all "Ireland, Ireland, Ireland." And then Jack asked me. I look back and say it was the best decision I ever made.'

The lounge is filling up now, the decibel level is rising fast and more people are eyeing him – which he either still doesn't notice or steadfastly ignores. His speech delivery, although at machine-gun speed and heavily accented, despite his decades away from his birthplace, remains audible. This stems, no doubt, from so many years of making himself heard to his fellow players on a football pitch surrounded by tens of thousands of baying fans, augmented latterly by ranks of bodhráns and roaring nostalgia for 'The Fields of Athenry'.

The decision to play with Ireland had to be a factor in leading to Ray Houghton's new and interesting career in the Irish media. 'I love this side of things, the media side. I love watching games – there isn't as much pressure. It's a really good company, RTÉ, they look after people who work for them, try to make them as welcome as they can, which does make a difference. Working for nice people, you want to do a good job. You'd pull the stops out – although [he laughs] if you were working purely for money you'd go elsewhere!'

In the context of the Irish broadcaster, he echoes the statement made by his fellow commentator Graeme Souness to Bill O'Herlihy about being allowed to tell it like it is. 'We can be a bit more opinionated. RTÉ is good at giving you your head, you can say what

World Cup USA, 1994.

you feel and as forcefully as you like, and if you get it wrong you put your hand up and say so and no one is going to pressure you.'

This has a lot to do with RTÉ's format but also with Ireland's small-nation status. 'It's a great format but you've got to understand we're not in the front line here. If you're in England, on Sky, ITV, BBC, you've got to talk to the chief execs, you've got to meet the managers, the pundits, the ex-players . . .'

The implication is clear. You'll want to interview them again so you have to be a little circumspect with your opinions, tone and line of questioning . . .

The current media landscape, utterly transformed over the span of Houghton's playing career, was brilliantly encapsulated by the *Irish Independent*'s Vincent Hogan when, during a radio interview, he described the depressing sight of large journalistic packs kicking their heels while 'waiting for teenage millionaires to come out and grunt at you before getting into their Porsches or Maseratis.'

'In years gone by you'd have one reporter from each newspaper, who, with pencil and notebook, assiduously and respectfully transcribed the thoughts of a player who felt privileged to be asked for them. You had three or four radio outlets, including networks, in Britain, now there are three or four thousand, each with at least three reporters at each significant match scrabbling to feed their instantaneous deadlines, with their mobiles and digital things. You're producing people to work in these places who've never really had the experience of the creativity of what it means to be a professional footballer.'

And speaking of the Porsche brigades, when he thinks back to what he was paid for his stints at West Ham, Oxford and Liverpool (five years, two hundred and two appearances, thirty-eight goals, two League and two FA Cup medals, with a reputation as a 'marauder' and 'creator'), does it hurt when he sees the mega-money being paid to top stars today?

He is sanguine, sees it as an inevitable evolution. 'We could all say that. When you look back at the fifties and sixties and see what they got, relative to us in the seventies and eighties, I feel sorry for them. Ten pound a week?

'Good luck to the lads today. The money's there. Make hay in the sunshine and have a fabulous lifestyle, that's what I say. These boys are never going to have to work again. All they have to decide is how to fill in the time. What country they're going to go to next week. What boats to buy and whatever – fair play.'

He is surprised to find himself working in the media. 'I always thought I'd be a manager, to be perfectly honest.' That he hasn't ascended these heights is actually a sore subject. 'I played with some great people in my time. Some of them went on to be managers and some of them who are managers are people I'd never have dreamed of becoming managers. Ever. Ever.'

He still wants it. So why doesn't he pursue it?

'That's a very good question. I think that people are looking for managers who are different. And not just personality-wise. In England at the minute you've got people who do off-the-wall things, Big Brother situations, in a House. "We're going to have a bonding session in my house. We've got four beds. You've got to vote who gets the four beds and the rest of you lie on the floor" – what's going on? It's a football team. How about trying 'em out to learn how to play the game? 'It's gone to ProZone and diet and blah blah.'

Bear with me, you anoraks, because this is new to me. ProZone, aimed at managers and coaches, is a piece of software based on a grid of the playing pitch. It analyses and collates data on individual and collective player movements, spewing them out along with statistics on tactical elements of the game. For Houghton that translates as 'You ran ten thousand metres last week, this week you've only run six thousand. There must be something wrong with you. You're not fit. Have you got an injury coming on?'

He doesn't dismiss this new-fangled stuff out of hand – for example, ProZone is an extraordinary boon for commentators and TV directors –'but none of this tells you when you stood still and let your mate go in for a goal. When you planned. When you thought strategically . . .'

When you watched and waited to pounce. When you employed the resources of your heart, memory, soul – and your courage. Notwithstanding, he continues to harbour 'a burning desire' to manage, although he accepts that 'It's no cake walk today. You're not just a manager, you're the dad. You have to look after these kids and wipe their backsides, even. Some of the players, they're ringing up managers because a light bulb is gone!'

This babying is not all that new; even in his own day players were not considered sensible enough to be in charge of their own passports. 'You'd have to go to the chief executive and ask him for it so you could go on holiday!'

Which is more important in a manager, respect or charisma?

'I think respect. Footballers today are very much looking at managers and asking, "What have you done?" If you have "done something", i.e. brought a team from nothing and have a trophy in the cabinet to show for it, you earn the respect of your players, which is vital.'

And if you're ticking boxes, you also need a guy who can deal mano-a-mano with the media. 'That's one of the modern problems. You have the close media attention and they can be very critical, maybe too critical.'

He instances the sarcasm and excoriation frequently meted out to Ireland's team, when 'there should be a bit of realism'. For example, Team England, with its 'huge personalities, players on huge contracts and with big heads, should be doing the best. But if they can't qualify, why should we expect our players to do it? Journalists have a job to do but they have to be a bit afraid of you. When Jack spoke, you could see them all going, "Uh-oh! Don't upset him!"' They had respect for the man as much as for the office he held. Sir Alex [Ferguson] had that as well. They had respect for him as a man, as a tough Glaswegian. Jack always protected his players, taking the pressure off. That's what he was great at. He was like the brick wall between the media and us – he wouldn't let them through. "Anything you got to say to them, you go through me!" he'd say, in his big booming voice.'

In conjunction with Big Jack's intractable self-belief, the voice and intimidating physical presence were used as artillery not only against the press pack but upstart players too. 'You wouldn't argue. You couldn't change Jack's mind as to how he wanted to play a game. If you said to Jack, "Well, what about trying this?"

'"No!" Before you got to the end of the sentence. You knew it was pointless.'

So, he echoes the criticism of Jack Charlton's managerial style that O'Herlihy, Dunphy and company have voiced?

Not fully. 'We had a reunion a couple of months ago. I was speaking to Kevin Moran and he was of the same opinion as I am, even more so. He said, "When you look back to 1988 and 1990, we could have done a lot better. Did we really believe in ourselves? Did we really give it as much of an opportunity as we could have?" And he was right.'

Houghton concedes that there is a certain logic in the contention that their team under Charlton was potentially great but didn't achieve this because their manager wouldn't trust them to play to their instincts – and full ability. There was method in Jack's edicts, though: 'He didn't want midfielders passing balls into midfield from the back,' and cited statistics that this was how most goals were given away.

'We were young – not in age but tournament-wise. We didn't know how international tournaments worked. And once you got into the opposition's third, your tackling third, he didn't care what you did. "You can do anything you want, doesn't bother me."'

By the time they got to USA '94, 'As a team we were really getting to the end. We were getting old together, we needed freshening up. And maybe we didn't do it quickly enough, didn't make the transition from older players.' As for the vanquishing of Italy in the Giants Stadium, 'You can always get one shock result, but over the campaign we didn't perform. We needed fresh legs.'

He misses it – and not just the big occasions. He misses the training, the camaraderie, and the sort of innocence.

Now he plays golf off a handicap of six, as competitively as if he were playing for a place on the Ryder Cup team. 'It's my passion now. The lower you get the more frustrated you get. I become very scientific about it – "paralysis by analysis", they call it.'

Just as Christy O'Connor Junior pulled out all the stops when playing golf with his sons, Houghton plays golf with his – and tries to slaughter them. He plays dominoes, darts or tiddly winks with twelve-year-old Harley and does everything in his power to slaughter her too. 'I gotta win.' He justifies this by saying, 'Kids need a good start in life. I don't want my kids to think it's easy – you gotta work hard to get on, you gotta earn it.'

So we can take it that Ray has a competitive streak, then?

He acknowledges it with a wry grin. Softens it. 'I'm a workaholic. Always been a grafter.'

To ask one of the most clichéd questions of all: what was the best game he has ever played?

Instead of a clichéd answer, he tells me how privileged he feels to have played in what some have termed 'The Game of the Century'. (That was the twentieth century – I Googled it later; the accolade is not his personal opinion.) In the clinking and braying cacophony of the Shelbourne tearoom, his voice lowers: 'There was one game where, as a team at Liverpool, we got great plaudits. We played Nottingham Forest and we beat them five–nil and the great Tom Finney said it was the greatest team performance he'd seen. That took a lot for someone to say. You don't get a phrase like that lightly.'

Up to this point he has been friendly but brisk, a little humorous, pretty factual. Now his eyes develop a shine and he looks younger than his forty-six years as he relives that night: 'Everything we did was perfection. It just felt like you were on auto-pilot. As though you were on the outside looking in.'

He compares that experience to his present role as omniscient commentator, or hurler on the ditch. 'Up there I never give the ball away, I'm the best player on the pitch. Someone does something, I'm like, "What're you doin'? It's simple!"

'That match was like that. Every decision made was the right one. None of us made a wrong decision, everyone was playing their A game, everyone was on the same frequency – it wasn't him on medium wave over there and I'm on long wave over here. Everyone was tuned in.'

I give him a second or two. Then, crassly, has he watched it on video?

He snaps out of soft focus. 'I'm sure there's a video of it but I'm not one to watch myself in the past. Someone says to me, "Oh, I bet you look at your medals all the time!" I never look at my medals. They're in a cabinet in the house. I'm not someone who puts jerseys up on the wall. I've got loads of shirts I've swapped. They're in a black bag in the loft.'

A man (this time definitely a banker or an accountant) is standing a little outside in the lobby and has clocked Houghton. He has excitedly pulled in another to confirm that, yes, it is him!

So what's Ray Houghton going to do to progress managerial ambition?

'Me best!' Another grin. (Both watchers in the doorway pretend to talk to each other.)

Listen, he must get bored answering the same questions, my questions, all the time?

'It does become repetitive, but the older you get the less it happens.'

The two watchers, dissappointed that they can't come in to the tearoom – it's full – leave. He doesn't escape, though. Because, as we're leaving the room, he's accosted once again – and again receives his fans and their memories with courtesy and good humour, as though he's hearing all this for the first time.

Listen, you people in the FAI! Will you give the man a testimonial? Seventy-three caps for Ireland? As you well know, he and John Aldridge (at sixty-nine caps) have even offered to share one, for God's sake.

And, by the way, Ray Houghton thoroughly enjoys *Après Match*, perhaps because he's not part of it. Not yet anyhow. It's probably because his hairstyle is too neat.

As a commentator, he'd probably appreciate the insertion here of a few more Colemanballs – for instance, this from our own Colm Murray, referring to the departure of Ireland manager, Brian Kerr: "His reign ended with that nil–all defeat by Switzerland at Lansdowne Road."

From a lady announcer on Manchester local radio: "And in the day's other football match, Manchester City and Norwich drew love–all.'

Or to put that the Scottish – i.e. the Houghton – way, from an announcer on Scottish TV: '. . .and with news of Scotland's nil–nil victory over Holland . . .'

Give the guy his bloody testimonial!

You'll Never
Walk Alone

Hillsborough

Ray Houghton was playing for Liverpool on 15 April 1989, one of the most tragically iconic days we remember, even though the death toll of ninety-six, the injury count of hundreds more and the incalculable legacy of emotional trauma for thousands upon thousands of men, women and children happened on the far side of the Irish Sea.

The match, against Nottingham Forest, was being played at the Sheffield Wednesday ground at Hillsborough. It was scheduled to start at three o'clock when, by some estimates, two thousand people or more were still trying to gain admittance to the venue.

It had always been predicted that at this match, Liverpool supporters would outnumber Nottingham's, yet the Merseysiders had been allocated thousands fewer tickets. Public warnings had been issued that fans without tickets should stay away. The warning went unheeded by some (although, subsequently, their turning up ticketless at the venue was considered by the Taylor Inquiry to have made only a minor contribution to the events that followed the punctual kick-off).

When the game began, the cheers of the crowds already inside fuelled the frenzy of the very large, rapidly congealing scrum of supporters still besieging the turnstiles. Latecomers – many, it has been reported, delayed by road works on one of the motorways leading to the venue – were arriving in droves, continuously augmenting the numbers.

*Previous:
Disaster strikes
during the FA Cup
semi-final match
between Liverpool
and Nottingham
Forest,
Hillsborough,
April 1989.*

The police were overwhelmed by the size of the shoving, jostling crowd and were, it seems, unable to cope. Fatally, in an effort to ease the logjam, the decision was made to open an exit gate nearby. This led to a mass dash through to the back of the already crammed terraces at the Leppings Lane end of the ground.

This large wave of new entrants pushed their way on to the terraces, creating a surge downwards against the intermediate barriers and the high, very strong fence erected to protect the pitch against invasion. The crowd on those terraces was so densely packed that those at the back had apparently no idea of what was happening in front of them as, adding to the problem, they struggled to see, over those in front of them, the action on the pitch.

As these events began to unfold, did Ray Houghton or any of his colleagues know how serious they were?

'No. No, we didn't. We were six minutes into the game. Peter Beardsley had taken a shot and he'd hit the crossbar. We knew there was something going on at the other end, at the Forest end, and all of a sudden there were fans running on the pitch. One of them came running up to me – "There's people dying down there . . ."'

Houghton, understandably, did not take this literally. English soccer hooliganism was at its height in the 1980s. 'My immediate reaction was that there was fighting going on down there, with both sets of fans getting at each other, and I was thinking, That's the last thing we need on a day like today, we've enough trouble.'

Unfortunately, the real trouble was only starting. That fence, erected to keep the crowds in, did its job too well. At least initially it held against the crush, except for a very small gap through which a number of fans managed to squeeze on to the pitch and safety. It

They'll never walk alone.

was when a policeman noticed this – and the efforts of some on the upper terrace to lift those below to safety – that he understood what was happening. He ran on to the pitch and ordered the referee to stop the game.

The referee obeyed, but even then neither he nor the footballers grasped what was happening. 'We were all called off the pitch. We were in the changing room, and the referee came in – as I'm sure he did to the Nottingham Forest players too – and he said, "Stay warm, lads. It won't be long until you're back out."'

And so 'for about thirty to thirty-five minutes', while people suffocated and died outside, the players, cocooned from hard information and frustrated at the delay, worked to keep their muscles supple. Houghton's group still believed that what was going on among the fans was merely a particularly rambunctious outbreak of scrapping between rival groups of supporters.

That was until dishevelled and distraught Liverpool fans started

Tribute on the pitch.

coming into their room and saying, 'There's people died out there!'

The atmosphere changed. Players panicked. 'Remember, these were the days when there were no mobile phones or anything and we all had family and friends at the game.'

Still they were not allowed on the pitch 'so we went upstairs and switched on BBC where on sports news [*Grandstand*] they were showing it, not exactly, but reporting what was going on. It showed people getting pulled up from the lower tier to the upper tier, people using advertising hoardings as makeshift stretchers. It was only then we realised. Up to then we hadn't a clue, really.'

With horrible irony, the same two clubs had met the previous year in the same stadium at the same stage of the same competition, with Liverpool afterwards lodging a complaint about overcrowding in the segregationist pens they had been allocated.

Most of the injuries and deaths on 15 April were from crushing and trampling. Many of the fans near pens, barriers and fences had died while pinned against them. Some had fallen. Some, while still standing, had died of asphyxia from the sheer press of numbers around them.

Football forgotten, the pitch now resembled a field hospital in the midst of war. With police, ambulance personnel and ordinary fans frantically working on the injured – or stretchering off the dead on anything they could use, including pieces of fence – the match was finally called off and the players were told to go home.

That night, Ray Houghton watched the unexpurgated horror unfold on *Match of the Day* and on every news bulletin on every channel. As did people in Ireland. And around the world.

Ninety-four people died that day. The ninety-fifth, Lee Nichol, fourteen years old, died four days later. The last to perish, the ninety-sixth casualty of the Hillsborough disaster, was Tony Bland, who spent almost four years in a coma; he died in March 1993.

Four days after the event, with the world in general and Liverpool in particular still coming to terms with what had happened, the semi-final of the European Cup was held between AC Milan and Real Madrid. Six minutes after the kick-off, the referee blew his whistle to signal a minute's silence in memory of the Hillsborough dead.

Half-way through this, at thirty seconds, the AC Milan fans began to sing softly, a swelling, heartfelt chorus of Liverpool Football Club's anthem: 'You'll Never Walk Alone'.

Because he has told the story of what happened at Hillsborough so many times, Ray Houghton's words sound well-aired but they do not sound well-worn. It is clear that, twenty-five years later, the feelings they engender are still raw. 'We didn't go back on the pitch for quite a while. There was no training, there was nothing. I think my first match after that was for Ireland against Spain.

'John Aldridge and I went to the first funeral with Kenny Dalglish. We went to quite a few. Two or three of the players went to every single one.

'Also, some of the families came to Liverpool. They just wanted to be around the club and see the players. They were coming in and they wanted to talk about football and they were telling stories about how they absolutely loved the club.

'We were sitting down and talking to them. Like counsellors, really, but we hadn't a clue what we were doing. We just knew it was best to be where we were, with the fans, talking. That was what the club was like. That's what Liverpool was like. The history and traditions there are phenomenal. It was their club. We were just the players. They'd supported us through thick and thin.'

Behind a slowly wilting wall of flowers, it was the players' turn to be the supporters.

Poppies in the Wind
The Christianity of Gordon Wilson

There were flowers in Enniskillen, lots of them, but not to excess: the people of that town are reserved. Do you remember 8 November 1987? Do you remember when, wearing poppies in remembrance of the young and middle-aged men who died in Flanders Fields, Ypres, Dunkirk and elsewhere, a group of Enniskillen townspeople stood around the cenotaph in their small town square, waiting decorously for their modest ceremony to begin?

I'm sure you remember that day when soldiers of the Provisional IRA had decided that their war for our freedom was a far, far better war to commemorate than any fought on foreign fields by Enniskillen's sons. Hiding the Enniskillen bomb behind the stout gable in a reading room was clever because when it blew out, the jagged, heavy rubble was sure to kill and injure lots of grocers and teachers and nurses.

The playwright Frank McGuinness had conceived his play *Observe the Sons of Ulster Marching Towards the Somme* while reading the names of the Inniskilling Fusiliers recorded on that war memorial. He confirmed that half, or more than half, of the names inscribed on it were of Catholics who had died in various world conflicts, incised without apartheid so that Spillane, McKernan, McCaffrey, Boyle, McKenna, Murray, Rooney, McBride, Malone, Montgomery, Nelson, Steenson and Threadkill were all equal in death.

Do you remember the name Gordon Wilson? Protestant. Born in Leitrim – Manorhamilton, actually. He had a grandfather ran a small farm at the foot of Benbo Mountain but apprenticed his son, Gordon's father, into the drapery trade. The father moved across the border to Enniskillen and opened a shop there, and when young Gordon, who'd been sent to Wesley College in Dublin, passed his Leaving Cert ('including Irish, I'm pleased to say') he joined the business. He ran Wilson's Drapery in the town for years. Soft-spoken, big spectacles. Businessman. Nice big house on a hill above the town. He became a senator in our Seanad down here, courtesy of Albert Reynolds. Tended to wear cardigans at home but a suit, naturally, when he was following the coffin of his daughter, Marie.

Previous: Poppy Day, Enniskillen, 1987.

He forgave Marie's killers. In front of microphones and cameras from all over the world, he said he would pray for them as he repeated his and Marie's story over and over: 'We were both thrown forward, rubble and stones and whatever, in and around and over us and under us.' Six feet of rubble, but it was a Sunday and nobody had a digger handy in the square at the time. They couldn't see each other but in the midst of the screams and the crying and the scrabbling above them as people tried to dig them out with bare hands, they were able to communicate every couple of minutes. 'Are you all right, Marie?'

'I'm all right.' Marie was twenty.

'I was aware of a pain in my right shoulder. I shouted to Marie

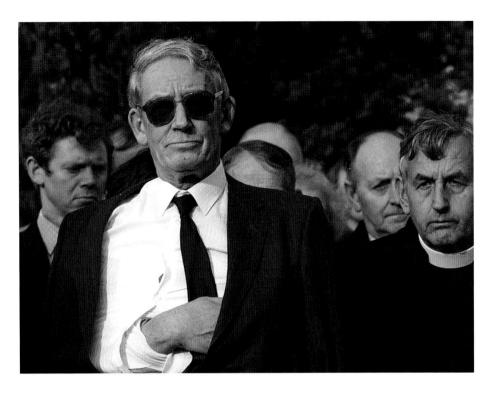

Gordon Wilson at his daughter Marie's funeral.

again, "Are you all right?" And she said, "Yes." She found my hand and said, "Is that your hand, Dad?"'

A chink of light. The rescuers seemed to be getting nearer.

Distant shouting. Was that an ambulance siren?

Thank God. 'Are you all right, Marie?'

'I'm all right.'

He was comforted. Marie was a nurse. She'd know when she was all right and when she wasn't.

Although at that point she was still alive under the rubble, Marie was the youngest to die that day. The other ten, Samuel Gault, Edward Armstrong, Kit 'Kitchener' Johnston and his wife, Jessie, Wesley and Bertha Armstrong, Alberta Quinton, Johnny Megaw, Bill and Nessie Mullan, were aged between forty-five and seventy-two. So, here we had three nurses, including Marie, an ambulance driver,

Nurse Marie Wilson.

one worker each from the Red Cross and the Salvation Army, a chemist, a telecommunications worker and two mothers.

Or, to put it another way, she'd been a daughter and murdered alongside her were five fathers, four mothers and a single, elderly man.

Somebody had found an iron bar and was using it to lever off the heavy rock and rubble. 'Are you all right, Marie?'

'I'm all right.'

Three or four times he asked her if she was all right and three or four times she told him she was.

Then the fifth time: 'Are you all right?'

The tone changed. 'Daddy, I love you very much.'

And although he continued to shout encouragement in her direction, that was the last he heard although she continued to hold his hand 'quite firmly', and after he was dug out and she was dug out after him, to be rushed to the Erne hospital, he still nurtured the hope that, young and healthy, she could survive this.

Marie's mother, as quiet as her husband and with no wish to vent her grief in public, described standing beside the hospital bed during the last few minutes of Marie Wilson's life. 'When I spoke, I saw her eyelids flicker. I will always see that. The sister in the ward turned to me and said, "Her heart has stopped beating." So the machine was switched off. We didn't know where to turn, it was just one of those things we will never forget. I turned to leave the room but I couldn't.

I kept coming back to look at her and going out and coming back.'

In the aftermath of the bombing, Gordon Wilson continued his patient recitals on radio: 'The hospital was magnificent, truly impressive, and our friends have been great, but I miss my daughter. We shall miss her but I bear no ill will, I bear no grudge. She was a great wee lassie, she loved her profession. She was a pet and she's dead. She's in heaven, and we'll meet again.

'Don't ask me, please, for a purpose. I don't have a purpose. I don't have an answer, but I know there has to be a plan. If I didn't think that, I would commit suicide. It's part of a greater plan, and God is good and we shall meet again.'

Each time he was asked, he reconfirmed that, every night, he would be praying for his daughter's murderers.

That first night, Remembrance Sunday night, as they drove home, having left their daughter's body behind in the Erne hospital, Gordon Wilson spoke to his stricken family. He asked them to handle the next few days 'with all the dignity we can muster'.

So that was what they did. Although he acknowledged that it was more difficult for some members of his family than for others, in memory of Marie they opened their home to family, friends and neighbours – and to strangers who, having heard him on radio, felt impelled to come to tell them how shocked they were and how they admired Gordon's lack of bitterness. A woman telephoned from the south to tell him she had been a life-long Republican but would no longer espouse that cause, 'and I can tell you some of my friends are with me'.

'And while I was on the telephone, a lady came into this house who I knew as what I would describe as a "hard-line Protestant". I knew that and she knew that, I knew that. And she said, "Gordon, you've done me a power of good. Your message has softened my heart."'

For the *Sunday Tribune*, I arrived in the town on the Wednesday.

Six victims were due to be buried that day; three, including Marie Wilson, had been buried the previous day and the last two funerals were to take place on the Thursday.

The Wednesday was wet and cold, with the type of wind chill that gets past the lining of the stoutest parka. In the empty square, yellow and white security tapes crackled around the bombsite, its grid of beams and rafters stark against the scudding clouds. A sodden fragment of paper poppy was stuck to the foundations of a railing and, with supreme irony, the statue of the soldier on top of

Marie Wilson's funeral, 1987.

the cenotaph's column, blind witness to the carnage, stood undamaged.

Such is the power of television – and the imagination – that it all seemed much smaller in scale than I had expected. Domestic.

It's the detail, stupid. So I recorded in my notebook that the first floor of the hall had collapsed, exposing the basement and its furnishings. On the top of a low cupboard stood a trayful of cheery red and yellow light bulbs. Not one had been damaged. A blackboard displayed the words 'PRIZES' and 'SNOWBALL' . . .

Outside the Methodist Church in Darling Street, twin hearses waited. Outside the Presbyterian Church in East Bridge Street, a second pair stood, and there were single hearses outside the High Kirk Presbyterian Church and the Garvary Parish Church.

I arrived at Darling Street, where Gordon Wilson and his wife, Joan, were already inside, as was a teenage boy, Julian Armstrong, who had been standing between his now dead parents at the time of the blast. One arm dangled by his side as if it was unusable, and in the grey light the scar on his head was livid. He had had to be supported into the church, past his parents' hearses and the overflow congregation.

As the service began, the wind tore the sound from the speakers installed outside the church but the people, despite struggling with blown-out umbrellas, joined in sober singing of 'Abide With Me', written by a man who had gone to Portora School down the road. They listened gravely as the congregation inside gave thanks for the lives of Julian's parents, Wesley and Bertha. With the strengthening wind sometimes obscuring the phrases issuing from the tinny loudspeakers, they strained to hear the words of reconciliation, hope and forgiveness from Wesley's brother, Bert.

These scenes were being replicated at the three other churches, as heard through the 'What stage are you at there?' crackle intermittently issuing from the walkie-talkie fixed to the lapel of an RUC constable nearby.

That evening, the weather was even colder but people left their snug houses in the euphoniously named Chanterhill and Rossory, Hollyhill, Castlecoole and The Brook. In response to unsigned leaflets dropped through their letterboxes calling them to a silent vigil, they walked from the Diamond to the cenotaph, treading respectfully around the hearse that had just delivered the latest victim to the Presbyterian church.

Although there were no obvious marshals or leaders, they formed a semi-circle in front of the bombed building, leaving a wide, half-moon space between themselves and the monument. A young woman read a passage from the Bible. A young man in a Salvation Army uniform stepped forwards, said a brief prayer and stepped back. The crowd then stood absolutely still and silent for five minutes. There was no coughing or shuffling, the only sounds being the howl of the gale in the blackened girders behind them, and the loud flapping of heavy plastic that covered some of the broken windows in buildings facing on to the square.

And then, again with no discernible signal, everyone dispersed.

They came back to East Bridge Street on Thursday afternoon, two thousand of them, to hear words of praise for two more of the good people of Enniskillen, Bill and Nessie Mullan. They heard the presiding minister read from Romans 12: 'Be joyful in hope, patient in affliction. Practise hospitality. Bless those who persecute you, bless and do not curse. Do not take revenge, my friends, but leave room for God's wrath, for it is written, It is Mine to avenge. I will repay, says the Lord. On the contrary, if your enemy is hungry, feed him. If he is thirsty, give him something to drink. In doing this you will heap burning coals on his head. Do not be overcome by evil but overcome evil by good.'

Afterwards, they walked behind the same two hearses that had carried Wesley and Bertha Armstrong the previous day.

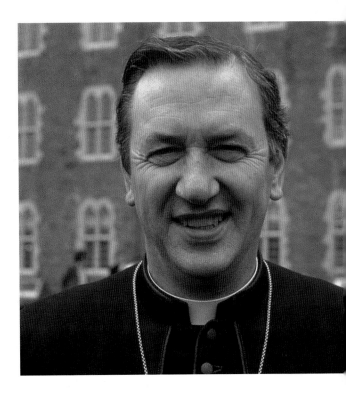

That evening, the Roman Catholic Bishop of Clogher held a service of reconciliation and repentance, and his church, too, was packed, leaving a huge, stoical and storm-battered overflow of Protestant and Catholic neighbours congregated outside to listen to him.

He told them, 'This was a moment of decision for all of us. The way of violence has failed us. Being ambiguous about violence has tightened the grip of real violence. We must now cut loose that grip at whatever cost to our pride or illusions. We must never again have to hang our heads in shame before the nations of the world.'

Bishop Joeseph Duffy of Clogher.

The Wilsons' home was still open to all, including those who intruded on their grief by 'just doing their jobs' with notebooks and tape-recorders. It was open even to some exceptionally rude members of the media, who talked with London accents, called them by their Christian names and dug through the ashes of their hearts for 'exclusives'. Sometimes there were three camera crews from three different TV companies in their house at the same time.

When I came to that house to be invited in, I walked through a hallway lined with boxes and boxes of mail from all over the world. The house telephone was ringing constantly, not only with requests for more media interviews – although that too – but with condolences and calls from 'ordinary' folk who had never met Gordon Wilson, were never likely to, but who just wanted to talk to him about how his words of reconciliation and love would for sure change the situation in the North.

At his core, though, Gordon Wilson was a practical man. He knew this atmosphere of goodwill would not burn at its present heat for ever: that the media would move on to the next buzz, that Northern Ireland would redraw its enemy lines. But he was also a Christian and believed that as a result of what he had reported – that his darling daughter's last words had been words of love – the lines might be softer and some vestige of finer feeling might blur the painters' hands. 'Hopefully it won't pass away in a week. Hopefully there won't be another tragedy. Hopefully, the message will get through that the answer is love.'

The late Cardinal Ó Fiaich and the Roman Catholic bishops of all Ireland combed through the files of previous post-atrocity statements in an effort to come up with something original and telling – something that would match the courage and Christianity of Gordon Wilson and make their own church's position as clear as possible. 'We spent a long time over it on the Monday in Maynooth,' said the cardinal. 'It was very carefully worded and very simply worded, so simply worded, I think, that to elaborate on any of the points made might only soften it and take from it.'

What was read at all Masses on Sunday, 15 November, one week after the Enniskillen atrocity, was solemn and clear.

There is no room for ambivalence. It is sinful to join organisations committed to violence or to remain in them. It is sinful to support such organisations or to call on others to support them.

It has become clear that dotted across this country there are safe-houses provided for members of these organisations.

There are people who store weapons or who willingly help fugitives to escape. We say very solemnly to these people that they share in the awful crime of murder. People must choose. There is no longer any room for romantic illusion. There is no excuse for thinking that the present violence in Ireland can be morally justified.

Not in the statement but in interview, Cardinal Ó Fiaich said further that IRA activists (or, in present terms, those in 'dissident' Republican organisations) 'can no longer consider themselves as practising Catholics'.

Cold comfort for Marie Wilson, but her father continued to live in faith, hope and love.

Despite statements from bishops and cardinals, the goodwill of the citizens of Enniskillen and many, many others, the skies did darken again. Change of heart is slow in Ireland. Ten and a half years passed, with many more funerals but, in truth, a small and sturdy seed had burrowed deep to germinate in the Irish psyche, and on Good Friday in April 1998, the Belfast Agreement was signed.

Gordon Wilson did not see it. He had followed his beloved daughter to their joint reward on 27 June 1995.

Had he lived on, to 26 April 2008, he would have felt gratified, perhaps justified, in clinging not only to hope but to his firm belief in redemption. Because that was the day that the Taoiseach of the Republic of Ireland, Bertie Ahern, stood before the United States Congress and the world formally to announce that Ireland was at peace.

Rooks and Their Nests

A Crucial Week in the Life of a Taoiseach

'Ireland is at peace.'

I defy anyone who heard those confident words, on a car or kitchen radio or a TV, not to have felt a jump in the blood. Bertie Ahern was acting as spokesman for many, many people, living and dead, whose decades-long efforts, not least his own, had culminated in the delivery of this triumphant sentence at a podium in front of the US legislators and the world.

He regards this speech as a much bigger deal than his address to the lords, ladies and MPs at Westminster a little earlier. For that one, 'I was over with Blair for a meeting that morning so I was relaxed enough. And we were in the middle of a general election so you were doing press briefings every day and everyone was roaring at you anyway, and everything was go-go-go.'

Taoiseach Bertie Ahern addresses a joint session of the US Congress in Washington, DC on April 30, 2008.

The event in Washington was different on many levels, including the formalities, and he was understandably somewhat daunted. 'We were in Nancy Pelosi's room [she is the Speaker of the House of Representatives] and she had gone in already and the reception party came out for me. And when you see all the big names, OK, Ted Kennedy and so on –' he waves a hand '– but when you see the others, John Kerry and all the Speakers, John Edwards, all the big world politicians . . . coming for me . . .'

He had not understood, until it was explained to him, why the public-address system was calling repeatedly for all meetings in the building to cease by eleven forty-five. 'I wonder why that's happening?' he asked conversationally, to be told that it was for him so that the House would be full.

He was astonished. 'Everything had to stop. No one would be allowed do anything else. Even if they were meeting a constituent . . .'

Dear God. Imagine! Not hearing out the complaints and requests of a constituent!

Anyhow, he and the reception party then 'took off with the Mace or whatever they call it over there. And all the staff came out into the corridor with me parading behind this Mace, and I kept meeting all these people who said, "Oh, we couldn't get in and we're third-generation Irish . . ."'

He had not reckoned on this parade, or on having to shake hands and greet his way through a maze of narrow corridors, so he was happy to reach the podium and be able to focus on the job in hand.

Of course he had rehearsed his speech thoroughly.

'Oh, yeah. That speech, I didn't really have to look down all that much, I had it well off. A speech like that you knew your punch lines. You hoped it'd work. The hardest part for us was the immigration bit. We knew that there was a danger of insulting them. We knew that there were differences between Republicans and Democrats. We knew that it was very important for the Irish.

'And when we got the applause for that – I wouldn't say it was the biggest applause in the world – but when we got the applause for that I was relieved. It was the most sensitive issue. If I didn't address it I might have felt I was dodging the issue. I could have said something about the war in Iraq and it would have been less controversial.'

And, of course, he had worked and worked again on that punch line about Ireland being at peace. He even secured help to punch it from Eoghan Harris, who advised him to count to six before he delivered that line. 'He was right. We all knew that "Ireland at peace" was the main punch line. But I didn't think it was going to punch as much. I think I was more pleased than anyone when I saw the whole place just, you know,' he chops upwards with his hands, 'j'dumph!'

That "j'dumph!" came more than ten years after the Good Friday Agreement. GFA. Seems like a long time ago now. Great day. Fully acknowledged by all.

After the celebrations, however, the cauldron of bickering, walkouts, shouting, protesting and slandering continued to bubble, steaming through what became known as ('the endless') Peace Process. So, who would have blamed a Martian for asking what all the happy fuss was about on that fine April evening in 1998?

As for us earthlings, given that many of the main players – Tony Blair, George Mitchell, Jonathan Powell and Alastair Campbell – have all written books about the thing, not to speak of the stories and books peddled by what seems like a million journalists, aren't we GFA'd to the point of stupefaction?

Maybe we are. Maybe we don't want to read any more about it.

Yet there is one central player who has not written a book (not yet anyhow) whose virtues of tenacity, ability to focus and patience led to that invitation from the US at last to deliver the unequivocal news. This is Bertie Ahern's story of a memorable week in 1998, of events that intertwined the professional and personal strands of his life in a truly extraordinary way.

Although, to put it mildly, the media consensus is that he is not blessed with narrative skills, the former Taoiseach's recollection of Good Friday Week, as he styles it, is clear and linear. His recounting will therefore be mostly in his own words, tweaked a little only for clarity and to cut out repetition. He has a verbal quirk I have not corrected because it probably mirrors the way he sees his public and private lives running in parallel, a state starkly highlighted by that Holy Week of 1998. He uses 'I' and 'you' interchangeably when referring to himself. I have corrected this only where it might cause confusion.

We meet in his new office suite, entered via an unprepossessing laneway at the back of a modern block, glass doors, state car with its engine ticking right outside. Although the Office of Public Works (I'm presuming here) has done its usual good job with the interior, the carpet is too new, the furniture too appropriate. Too many gaps on the walls, too few bits of bog oak and souvenirs of triumphs past. This has been quite a hasty lash-up.

Opposite:
A sign of things to
come, 1983.

Relaxed, pink shirt, dark suit, Bertie is sanguine about his new, humbler status. 'In good form, yeah. I'll be busy for a month more. Overlapping things. Things I was to do for people in the autumn brought forward. And the tribunal and so on.' It's dropped in casually. (We are meeting on Tuesday, 3 June. He is due back in Dublin Castle the following day but the focus of this interview has been defined – by me when making the request for it; it is not to add to the tons of analysis or questioning on that situation.) 'So until I'm finished all that I won't be able to start getting myself into order . . .'

He has yet to read Jonathan's book but wasn't mad about Alastair's. 'It's more what he left out rather than what he left in. He left out what was embarrassing to the Labour Party. I went through it because I wanted to see stuff I was interested in and I could find none of it.'

Tape-recorder between us, we sit kitty- corner to one another at the blondish, unmarked table. His posture is open, legs apart, one arm dangling loosely. 'We had prepared for months for what would be the last week. And when we came into that last week . . .'

Here we go . . .

Ah, no, not quite yet.

'The previous week was horrendous because there were huge difficulties and differences.'

Tony Blair was distracted by his chairmanship of an important Asian-European summit in London, so Bertie had to take on an extra travel load, flipping over and back between London and Dublin: 'I'd spent most of that week, each morning and each evening, dealing with him and George Mitchell, trying to get us lined up for the week. I came back to Dublin on the Saturday. The whole week – that Good Friday week – was to start on the Sunday. The deadline George Mitchell had set was that we would finish on Holy Thursday. Midnight.'

Gethsemane.

We are quietly joined by Mandy Johnston, the ex-Taoiseach's aide. I believe at first that she is there to monitor the questions – and worry briefly – but as it turns out, there was no need for alarm. Afterwards, she tells me that since she had read and heard only passing references to the personal element of this historic week, she was merely interested in the sequence. Three times during the hour, and three times only, he turns to her, once for affirmation of something he'd said, twice to prompt him for a name that has slipped his mind.

So, Holy Thursday the deadline was. That was definite. And so confident were they of the making (or final breaking) over that Last Supper that all sides had made Easter weekend and bank-holiday plans – all the delegations and public servants and political advisers and the three and a half thousand journalists registered in Belfast.

All bound for a bit of R and R after what seemed like a lifetime of wearisome bi-laterals and tri-laterals, nay-saying and demands for clarification. Bertie himself was bound for Kerry. Gagging, he was, for the pure air and the familiar tang of the sea. 'It was a very clear buffer. And it wasn't that it might go over. We knew we had to finish on that Thursday.'

OK. On the Sunday, the first day of the week, he arranged to have a series of briefing meetings with the political parties. 'It started off in the typical sense in that the first party didn't turn up.' But instead of taking advantage of the unexpected free time, 'I stayed in St Luke's, doodling around for a few hours and didn't go up to Church Avenue, which I normally would do on a Sunday.'

St Luke's is in Drumcondra. His mother lived on Church Avenue, not far away. He decided to postpone the visit and to go up to her later in the day. 'It's the one huge regret I have. When I was doing nothing I should have gone up but I didn't, unfortunately. Because if I'd gone up to Church Avenue I'd have found that my mother wasn't well.'

Unknowing, he left St Luke's for Government Buildings to preside over his next meeting, this one with the SDLP delegation, who did turn up. He was in the middle of this when 'I got a call that my ma had taken a heart-attack.'

The shock was profound. 'But I'd a meeting with the UDP and the others after that, so I couldn't leave. They'd all come down from Belfast so I just couldn't. I had to keep going with the meetings. But at least I rang my brothers to make sure they were there with her.'

He did take advantage of the lunchtime break.

'I remember at lunchtime that day, I was to go out to do a thing for Bronwyn Conroy. So I said to the others, "Listen, you all have lunch," and I went out and did the thing for Bronwyn Conroy and said nothing, and then I went straight to the Mater to find that Mam was still alive, but it was very clear straight away that she was in trouble.'

Up to this his tone has been brisk but this is mumbled to the floor. He recovers quickly: 'I went back to the meetings, and then when the meetings finished, I think about teatime, I went up to the Mater and stayed until about six a.m. She died on the Monday morning.'

That Monday, he had made a prior arrangement to brief the Republic's parties and to copper-fasten the final position before leaving for Hillsborough. 'And, of course, word had broken on the eight o'clock news and so on, and they all thought I'd cancel, but there was no way I could cancel because the week was on the deadline. The only day of that week I was staying in Dublin was on that Monday.

'So I had to go over and spend a few hours with Fine Gael and Labour and they all appreciated that I was doing that and so on, but I had to do that.'

All through the Sunday and the Monday, even as he listened and debated during probably the most important meetings of his life, the words, 'Why didn't I go up to Church Avenue? Why didn't I go up to Church Avenue?' beat like a punishing drumbeat in his mind. 'What I did then, on the Monday night, I went up to the Mater. Because I said to myself, "Jeez, me ma's dead and here I'm going to be gone half the week." I went up and said to the nuns, "Look, do you know what I want to do? I want you to use the keys to open the morgue and let me alone." And they did that. They would have moved her into another room if I'd have wanted it. But I didn't want that. I turned on no light, nothing. It was just the morgue as it would normally be at night.'

For three hours, from eight in the evening to eleven, he sat by his mother's side in that still, silent darkness. Not just the two of them, however. There were, he thinks, about five other bodies lying there with them. 'I don't actually know how I did it because the normal thing is that when I go into a morgue the only thing I want to do is to get out. But it was actually good. It was satisfying. Because when I came out of there I was actually quite happy. I remember I met some of my friends and we went for a pint. It felt good that I did it. Because to this day I say, "Why didn't I go up on the Sunday morning?" I was mad I didn't. I still am mad I didn't.'

For the next few days, his feet barely touched the ground. 'On the Tuesday I had to go to the North for the preliminaries of that week, and then I was back down for the removal from the Mater to Marino Church. Didn't go back up on the Tuesday night and I said, "That's great now, the funeral is in Marino at twelve o'clock and after that, then, I'll be able to go back up to Belfast."'

And have a bit of sleep, maybe?

Well, no.

'When I left Marino Church that night on the Tuesday I was met by my own officials from the Taoiseach's Department and by the foreign affairs guys to tell me that the whole thing was in danger of collapsing and there'd been a major mess-up, and blah, blah, and they really, really needed me to talk to George Mitchell urgently, and to talk to Tony Blair urgently.

'And I remember very well sitting on the wall of Marino primary school on Griffith Avenue, talking to Blair and talking to George Mitchell and back to Blair and back to George Mitchell.'

Bertie began to walk. 'George Mitchell records this very well in his book. I rang him four or five times forward and back, and he kept saying, "Where are you?" and I kept saying, "Griffith Avenue," and he'd say, "How could you be still on Griffith Avenue?" The reason is, I was walking on my own, minus security – I don't know how I got rid of security but I did. Anyway, I walked from Marino Church, all the way to Mobhi Road, across Mobhi Road . . .'

Including Griffith Avenue Extension?

'Including Griffith Avenue Extension and all the way back to the church, ringing George Mitchell and ringing Blair back and ringing my own gang back and forth. George couldn't understand this. It was nine o'clock and it was half nine and it was ten o'clock and it was half ten and he's still on Griffith Avenue? He knew I was walking because he could hear the cars. He said in his book, "I thought he was walking all over Dublin."'

The good senator had not quite plumbed the depths of Bertie's loyalty to his constituency and its loyalty to him. He was so intent on his phone calls that evening he didn't notice what attention he was attracting from passers-by but concedes that people were probably looking at him all right. 'I'd say they were. Everyone'd know you on Griffith Avenue, running and jogging.' His people were no doubt unwilling to interrupt what was obviously important business, even to condole.

Where does he get his patience? How does he endure? 'Hard to explain. Whether it's a strike or whatever, you try to work out at the start what it is you're trying to achieve. The long ball. My early days negotiating with trade unions and strikes and so on, you couldn't pay any of the extra money because it was outside the guidelines; but you didn't want to crack the unions into an us-and-them Thatcherite thing – so what was the objective? And if in the middle of all of that there's abuse and rancour, well, you just have to take it as par for the course. It won't happen overnight. You take nothing personally. They hit you with the sword, you just have to take it on the chin and move on all the time.'

Is there such an animal as a thin-skinned politician?

'Oh, yeah.' He is surprised by the question. 'Lots of them. Actually, most of them. My rule of thumb is you can say, almost without exception, that those who give it are the worst at taking it. That's my experience over the years. I'm not going to mention any names.'

Ah, go on!

Across the table from Sinn Féin: Ash Wednesday, 1 March, 2006.

He laughs. 'Those who give it are very poor at taking it. The exception to that rule was Charlie Haughey. He was good at giving it but did take it . . .'

Anyhow, to get back to the outcome of that long walk up and down Griffith Avenue: 'The politics was that I had to go up to Belfast the following morning to have this breakfast meeting in Hillsborough to try to get our negotiating position correct and the whole thing back on the rails. I was late in bed – actually I didn't see much of my bed that whole week. I'd seen none of it on the Sunday, I'd seen a bit of it on the Monday, this is Tuesday and we've to go up north at some unearthly hour in the dawn. Five or five thirty. I think the breakfast meeting was seven or seven thirty, where they met for about an hour and a half with Mitchell and Blair and then I had to go and meet the Shinners, and then the SDLP, just to get the Nationalist side on. And fly straight back down, and I just got to Church Avenue before the family left to go to Marino Church. I remember coming in and I remember going out in the back garden with the family and we all left from there.

'The funeral went on for ever. The archbishop kindly said the Mass but I'd decided not to speak. I'd said to my brother, Maurice, I'd just sit back. It was quite a nice ceremony but a long ceremony. There were a whole lot of musicians of all kinds, Paddy Cole, who my mother loved, the Diocesan Choir, who knew my father from All Hallows [Bertie's father worked for the Diocesan College in Drumcondra] and our friend who sings always on Remembrance Day in the Royal Hospital.' Bernadette Greevy.

'And I remember the Archbishop saying, "We wish the Taoiseach well with the negotiations."'

This was, he indicates, a jolt. In the hothouse atmosphere in which he existed at that time, he was only barely conscious that the media – pulling the population in its wake – was avidly following every breath, every tick and tock of the negotiations. 'I hadn't listened to any of the news. I don't listen to the media when I'm involved in things. Mandy'll tell you. I never do.' He looks across at Mandy, who nods.

So we are at the Wednesday afternoon now and the number of hours of proper sleep that the Taoiseach had enjoyed since the previous Saturday night could probably have been counted on the fingers of one hand and a couple of extra thumbs. As the shots were fired over his mother's grave, there must have been a surreal, even hallucinatory quality to his own existence at that point?

'I was tired, yeah. I was thinking of my ma dying and thinking of the week that was and thinking, Jeez, this is a crazy week.' And right on cue, as the thought occurred, 'I remember turning around in the graveyard and somebody saying to me, "Sorry, we really have to go, we have to head for the airport. I felt a bit mad. I felt, Jeez, this is terrible, they're all going back now to the Skylon [Hotel] and I can't.'

The demands on him were apologetic but insistent, and he had no alternative but to give in. Although in his temporary absences the talks up north had continued, 'They were saying to me that they'd tic-tac and keep things going until I got back, and I was conscious that nothing too much was going to happen. At the same time you realised that you had a job and you had to do your bloody job. There was no way I could turn around and say I'm not going.

'The problem in the North the whole way through – and it continued for years – because I was involved with it for so long and all the shots were being made by me and the stakes at that time were very high and it was all about Articles Two and Three and the Constitution and people were saying I was negotiating them away – nobody in the system, nobody, would make any decision.

'Lots of times in politics you'd have civil servants doing this and that, running the Taoiseach and running the ministers, but I was very conscious all the time that with the North, nobody did anything until you did it. In the Good Friday talks, it was the one time in my life – maybe the European Constitution was the other, when we were negotiating that – nobody would make any decision.

'So what I did was I went up to the Skylon and I shook hands with everybody, they were all up to have a meal there, and then I went straight to the airport. That's how me poor mother, and her funeral, got immersed in it.'

He was in 'very bad humour' when he arrived back at Castle Buildings, but then 'a lovely thing' happened. In deference to his bereavement, 'the journalists all had agreed that when I came in everybody would put down their cameras. Both the still cameras and the TV cameras. The senior fella, Mouth Almighty up there [Eamon Maillie, name confirmed by Mandy] got up on a ladder and made a speech to the assembled press, talking for all three and a half thousand of them. They'd made this gesture and they wanted to tell me that they'd great admiration for me. It was lovely. So much so that afterwards I said I'd love to get a photograph of that occasion. And to this day I haven't been able to get a photograph. Everybody respected it. Three and a half thousand journalists and there wasn't one photograph. Which was extraordinary.

'So when I give out about journalists at other times, I have to say that that day, it was remarkable.'

That was at about four o'clock on the Wednesday.

'So we went in and we got on with the talks, which ran until about midnight.'

Bed then? Remembering that he had left Dublin at about half past five that morning for his first round of negotiations? And had buried his mother before flying up again?

Well, no. 'Everyone said they were going to bed but I had a thing about Belfast at that time that I wouldn't stay there. I'd always come back.'

Eh?

'Just had a thing about it. They wanted us to stay in Hillsborough. I just had a hang-up about that, so I wouldn't stay.'

He flew back to Dublin and, of course, the funeral party had long dispersed. 'Everyone was long gone to bed. I don't think I slept very well so I got up and went for a dawn walk in All Hallows.'

And then he went back up to Hillsborough and joined the breakfast meeting on the Thursday morning for the final countdown. The talks started at nine o'clock.

Those last talks went right through and into the night, all night, until they finished at five o'clock on the Friday afternoon. 'That was right through, one go. No stop.' His only stop in those negotiations was that, unknown to everyone 'except one security guy', Bertie did a flit to attend a Holy Week service. 'I managed to get out to some church where everyone nearly dropped dead when they saw me. I can't remember where it was, Castlegormley or somewhere.'

He escaped again during the Friday, to a different church, but this time 'there was a good few of them with me because they didn't want to let me out of their sight'.

What he remembers, as Holy Thursday and Good Friday became indistinguishable on clock faces, is that 'when we got into the night, Sinn Féin had a whole lot of issues. Everyone had a whole lot of issues, but Sinn Féin had a whole lot of unanswered questions. At

'My girls.'
With Cecelia
and Georgina.

that stage there wasn't a whole lot of contact between the Brits and Sinn Féin. We tended to do that through the Irish government.'

Bertie's team, who included David Andrews and Liz O'Donnell, were conducting series of meetings with all the parties. 'I was handling the Sinn Féin list and the UUP list. They were the two I saw the difficulties with. But there were also bi-laterals – we had Sinn Féin talking with the SDLP.'

To add to this verbal din, outside Castle Buildings, breath clouding in the frosty air, the DUP and the PUP were 'shouting and roaring' at the negotiators and, it seemed, at the world in general. 'And that went on until about eleven o'clock at night, which was kind of entertaining!'

Throughout that Thursday night, the Irish delegation worked with 'poor old Mo [Mowlam, Secretary of State for Northern Ireland and now deceased], trying to narrow down the list, tick as much of the boxes as possible. And I was doing the direct negotiations with Sinn Féin, then going back to the Brits and trying to negotiate with them'.

They came to the 'difficult issues, prisoners and so on' at, he thinks, somewhere between five and six on the Friday morning. But before they jumped in, Bertie needed a lungful of fresh air and so, with a few of his officials, he went out through the security door into the gardens of Castle Buildings.

There then occurred another of those situations that, given the circumstances, was perfectly surreal.

It had been snowing and the air outside was not only cold but raucous with the calls of a waking rook colony. Instantly our Taoiseach took it upon himself to 'explain to the guys about the nests and why they build their nests all together'.

Light stole into the eastern sky as the enthralled but novice twitchers strained their necks to peer into the branches while the Bert went enthusiastically into detail, explaining that the wheeling, croaking birds had 'this family thing where they all go to the one tree so they won't get attacked and so on . . .'

Crunch! Crunch! It's the tramp of Philistine feet. The RUC. Machine-guns at the ready. 'To try and find out what these half-nutty fellas were doin' out in the snow at the crack of dawn watching rooks building nests . . .

'After we went back in there were crucial negotiations with Blair and the Shinners. Blair hadn't had much dealings with the Shinners at that stage – at a later stage there were millions – but at that stage he hadn't. So I'd say while a lot of the others were still asleep, from about six in the morning to about ten, we had some of the most crucial meetings. They went well, in my view.

'And we came out of that and went straight into negotiations with [Jeffrey] Donaldson and [David] Trimble, which were very difficult. Because Donaldson walked out on Trimble. That went on until lunchtime. I thought it had gone well except for Donaldson not being on side.'

Finally! Bertie, George and Tony have signed the Good Friday Agreement, April 10, 1998.

As we already know, Bertie left them all to it and went at three to the religious service, when the result of all this work was still 'clearly in the balance. We had finished the negotiations, effectively, and it was clearly a question now as to whether Trimble would come along with it.' The decree was that everyone had to have reported in to George Mitchell before five o'clock.

When Bertie returned, David Trimble still had not reported in. 'We had a session with Mitchell. And then Trimble indicated that he'd go with it and we arranged the meeting. One square table with everybody, where everybody indicated they were in agreement. It was short and sharp.'

That final meeting was 'a great session. Great atmosphere where Mitchell asked everyone if they'd sign up. Sinn Féin said of course they couldn't sign up on behalf of the IRA but that the IRA weren't objecting.'

The actual signing ceremony was brief, just Tony Blair and himself; the two then gave a short press conference where they read statements. 'I was wearing a black tie. The two of us looked pretty wrecked.

'Then all hell broke loose. The world media went gaga. It was a world story and everybody was shaking hands with everybody and it was quite a nice day, cold but a nice day, beautiful, everybody was outside and there was this huge thing, with everyone signing everyone else's brochure, but to be honest, as soon as it was done I immediately switched. Any of those clips – and I've seen millions of those clips with everyone shaking hands and signing things – I'm not in any of them.'

The story falters here and it's not hard to guess why. *The Week* had caught up with Bertie Ahern. He gave just one interview, to RTÉ (after he got back to Dublin he gave another to a *Prime Time* special), and went quietly back upstairs to collect his notes. While there, he remembers the civil servants in the North asking him, '"Will you sign this? And will you sign that?" and I did. I signed a lot of things.' He also remembers, 'and this was caught on camera, John Taylor came over and thanked me on behalf of the Unionists, coming up here with me mother's funeral and all that. Which was nice of him.'

After Taylor had left, Bertie stood silently by the window for a few moments to watch what was happening below on the green. 'They were all hugging each other and shaking hands and taking photographs of each other.' He and his colleagues departed for Dublin soon after.

When they boarded the Air Corps plane, things looked up: he was chuffed to find that champagne had been laid on.

And here is an interesting aspect of the double life he led that week; it echoes the jolt he felt on hearing the Archbishop's good wishes for the negotiations from behind his ma's coffin. 'I got back to Dublin airport and found half the parliamentary party was there and all the family were there and half the people who were at the funeral were there and half the country seemed to be there, all cheering.' It was only then he realised fully 'that people were following this. People were up at three in the morning. Up all night . . .'

So, greetings and cheering over. Bed then?

Not yet. He and his crowd met again in St Luke's. 'And the President rang me. And Ted Kennedy rang me. They're the two I remember.'

Sense of achievement, now, surely?

He considers this. 'It was at that stage when the President and Ted Kennedy rang me, when the President, as she always would do, made it seem as if it was huge . . . Because as soon as the thing was over, I just wanted to get back, to check how me sisters were and how the family were. The only thing I thought of was home. In fact I turned my mind totally – I just wanted to get home. I didn't realise they'd all be at the airport, which was dead handy.

'Remember, from the Sunday morning, from the time my mother took the heart-attack, other than the Sunday night Monday morning when she died, I'd hardly seen them. From the graveside I hadn't been able to go to the afters or anything. I hadn't even talked to them. I'd talked to my girls all right. I talked to my girls on the Friday morning . . .'

He considers again. 'I had to finish it. The last conversation I had with my mother, it was about the Good Friday agreement. She said, "Do you think you're going to succeed on this?" And she was wondering about Articles Two and Three because my mother would have been quite political.'

It's a delicate way of putting that his mother, Julia, a West Cork woman from Castledullivan, just outside Bantry, held serious Republican views and had mixed feelings about the removal of Articles Two and Three from the Irish Constitution. 'Yeah, my mother's area was Fine Gael but she and her family were diehard Republican. Both my parents [Bertie's father was from near Kinsale] were political. Both hated the Brits, hated the Tans. My mother didn't have much time for anything to do with the Brits, football, sport, anything.' The implication is that Julia Ahern had swallowed her principles for the sake of the country. And her Bertie. She made her departure, however, before the deed was actually done.

'So it was on my mind that it would be good if I could get this through, if I could finish it.'

He finished it, and the President made a huge thing of it, and here he was with his family and friends in St Luke's, but because it was Good Friday, none of the pubs was open. So they just hung around in St Luke's, he says, 'for a while. An hour or so,' and then he went home to bed. Finally.

It was dawning on him 'in bits and pieces, that this thing really was huge. I was saying to myself, "Jeez, this does mean something." I hadn't read any of the Irish media – no, that's not true, I'd read one editorial. Paddy Duffy rang me on the Saturday morning and he said, "Would you believe it, the *Irish Times* has managed to run a front-

page editorial and not mention you?" So I did read that. And I said to meself, "It's only the *Irish Times* could do that."'

There was something else to finish, complicated yet again by the surreal contrasts that had marked out the entire week.

On the Saturday, Bertie and his family went back to Church Avenue. 'The family gave me the honour of reading my mother's letters that she'd sealed, because I was the youngest and not because I was Taoiseach, which I was quite chuffed about.'

It was a moving occasion, naturally, and when he had finished reading them, everyone was broken-hearted. 'I was very upset too, but Kofi Annan rang on the home phone number. So the reason I wasn't crying with all the others was I had to pull meself together and go out and talk to Kofi Annan!'

Job done: man in shadow.

Next page:
Parity of esteem.
Italia '90, Ireland 1,
England 1, Cagliari.

Acknowledgements

I would like to express profound gratitude to the interviewees around whose memories of events I have based most of this book. So, very sincerely, I thank Bertie Ahern, Gillian Bowler, Gay Byrne, Moya Doherty, Ray Houghton, Johnny Logan, Charlie McCreevy, Tom McSweeney, Bishop John Magee, Mike Murphy, Christy O'Connor Junior, Kevin O'Connor and Bill O'Herlihy. My interview with the late Gordon Wilson was conducted when the Enniskillen bombing and the death of his daughter, Marie, had occurred only days before and so I must record here how gracious he was to me in the midst of such chaos and personal tragedy.

Thank you, Pat Neary, for help in negotiating the mysterious planet of golf. For their time and trouble in finding information – and help in setting up the interviews – gratitude is owed to Mona McGarry, Ailis Sherrard, Ann O'Connor, Justin Healy, John McColgan, Carol Cronin, Declan and Mary Purcell, Maurice Ahern and Sandra Cullagh.

Gratitude to those who helped with background reading and conversations. For instance, some additional facts for the piece on the visit of John Paul II to Ireland were gleaned from articles by Joe Carroll of the *Irish Times*, from the personal experience of Kevin Healy, and from two books: *Green is My Sky* by the late Aer Lingus Captain, Aidan Quigley, and *His Holiness*, by Carl Bernstein and Marco Politi. Charlie Bird's memoir *This is Charlie Bird* prompted my own recollections of the Stardust fire tragedy. And in the archives of the *Examiner*, Caroline O'Doherty's account of the death of Ann Lovett and her baby brought back the horrors they went through. I acknowledge also those who run the websites and archives not only of the *Examiner*, but of the BBC, RTÉ, *Irish Independent* and *Irish Times*. Special thanks to the Murphy family for their holiday snap! And thanks to Tom Banahan of Banahan McManus Advertising for his help with the Budget Travel archive.

I am grateful to my agent, Clare Alexander, and to the Hachette Books Ireland friends who have kept the faith: Breda Purdue, my editor Ciara Considine, Claire Rourke, Ciara Doorley, Ruth Shern, Peter McNulty and Jim Binchy. Many thanks also to book designer Sinéad McKenna.

For their continuing interest and staunch encouragement I thank from the bottom of my heart a large corps of loyal friends and colleagues, old and new. I thank Patsy McKeon and my kind and generous Bramblewood neighbours too.

And hey, Kevin, Adrian and Simon! I love you dearly.

Deirdre Purcell
19 September, 2008

Permissions Acknowledgements

The author and publisher would like to thank the following for kind permission to reproduce images:

Alamy Images: X, 17.

Banahan McManus: 120, 133.

Corbis: VII–IX, 3, 167, 168–169.

Dublin City Library Archive: 144.

Getty Images: II–(Dana, Bono and Houghton), 6, 38, 42, 78, 98–99, 113, 116, 118, 122, 126, 167, 168-169, 181, 190, 219, 222, 230–231, 233, 234, 250, 267, 272.

Inpho Photography: 189, 208, 215.

Irish Examiner: 175.

Irish Times: XIV, 9, 20–21, 22, 27, 33, 85, 180, 182, 255, 265, 271.

Johnny Logan: 82, 88, 95.

National Library of Ireland: 154.

Pa Photos: 178, 206, 212–213, 216.

Pacemaker: II (Enniskillen), 238–239, 241, 242, 244.

Phil Sheldon: 106.

Photocall Ireland: 45, 62, 65, 71, 136, 139, 156, 159, 184, 203, 261.

RTÉ: 12–13, 30, 33, 34, 35, 56–57, 59, 68, 76, 80, 140, 145, 147, 148–149, 160–161, 172, 191, 196, 247.

Sportpixs UK: 110.

TopFoto: 103.

For permission to quote from his song 'Dancing with My Father', the author and publisher would like to thank Johnny Logan.

Every effort has been made to fulfil requirements with regard to reproducing copyright material. The author and publisher will be glad to rectify any omissions at the earliest opportunity.